Charting Change

Previous Publications

Stoking Your Innovation Bonfire, 2010
Contributing Author to *A Guide to Open Innovation and Crowdsourcing*,
 edited by Paul Sloane, 2011

Charting Change

A Visual Toolkit for Making Change Stick

Braden Kelley

Illustrated by
Kathy Kelley and Gabriella Kelley

palgrave
macmillan

First published 2016 by
PALGRAVE MACMILLAN

The author has asserted their right to be identified as the author of this
work in accordance with the Copyright, Designs and Patents Act 1988.

Palgrave Macmillan in the UK is an imprint of Macmillan Publishers
Limited, registered in England, company number 785998, of Houndmills,
Basingstoke, Hampshire, RG21 6XS.

Palgrave Macmillan in the US is a division of Nature America, Inc., One
New York Plaza, Suite 4500, New York, NY 10004-1562.

Palgrave Macmillan is the global academic imprint of the above companies
and has companies and representatives throughout the world.

Hardback ISBN: 978–1–137–53695–2
E-PUB ISBN: 978–1–137–53696–9
E-PDF ISBN: 978–1–137–53697–6
DOI: 10.1057/9781137536976

Distribution in the UK, Europe and the rest of the world is by Palgrave
Macmillan®, a division of Macmillan Publishers Limited, registered in
England, company number 785998, of Houndmills, Basingstoke,
Hampshire RG21 6XS.

Library of Congress Cataloging-in-Publication Data

Kelley, Braden, author.
    Charting change : a visual toolkit for making change stick / Braden
  Kelley ; illustrated by Kathy Kelley and Gabriella Kelley.
      pages cm
    Includes bibliographical references and index.
    ISBN 978–1–137–53695–2 (alk. paper)
      1. Organizational change. I. Title.
HD58.8.K4577 2016
658.4'06—dc23   2015033525

A catalogue record for the book is available from the British Library.

This book is dedicated to the men and women who recognize that everyone changes the world every day, embrace that fact, and commit their lives to making that change a positive one.

Contents

Figures

Preface

The idea for this book came to me in a dream and started to take shape shortly thereafter. The core idea is that change is accelerating and organizations need to become more agile and more capable of continuous change. This presents a huge challenge for most organizations.

Let's face it: Initiating change is a scary, overwhelming process that we often try to avoid because we lack the tools to make the process more collaborative and visual and manageable. We lack tools to help us organize the desired change in a way that guides a group of people through the change planning process, accumulating buy-in and an understanding of what it will take to execute the change.

What emerged from this dream is a collaborative, visual Change Planning Toolkit™ that is composed of:

- a set of new methodologies and frameworks to simplify complex change concepts and help people better structure their organizations and their efforts to support change;
- the Change Planning Canvas™ (see figure P1.1) which will help managers get everyone literally all on the same page for change;
- a set of worksheets designed to lead people one topic at a time toward a completed Change Planning Canvas™.

A completed Change Planning Canvas™ will give more visual, agile organizations everything they need to move from planning to execution. Organizations that are more process intensive will have everything they need to easily build a set of change plans containing any additional specifics required as inputs into their change process.

In the chapters that follow we will discuss:

- a selection of the best practices of organizational change;
- ways in which the best practices of change management and project management need to change;
- ways to effectively plan your change using components of the Change Planning Toolkit™.

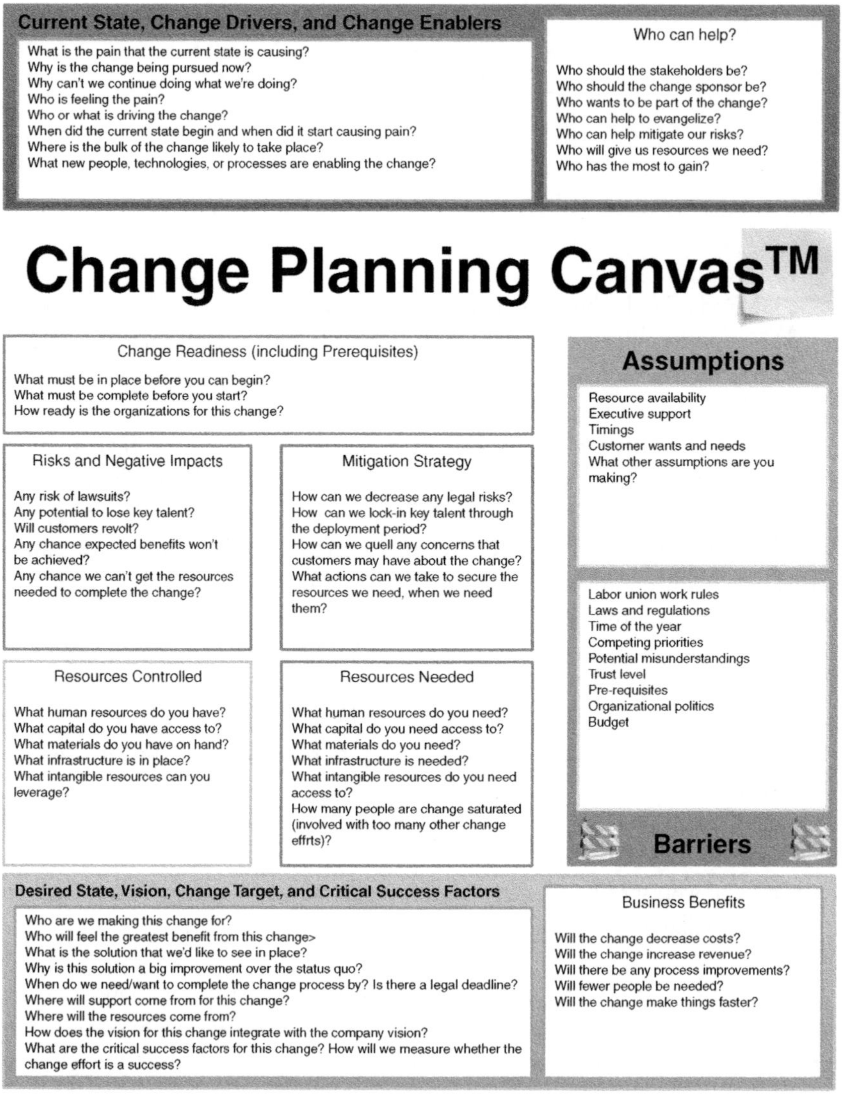

Current State, Change Drivers, and Change Enablers

What is the pain that the current state is causing?
Why is the change being pursued now?
Why can't we continue doing what we're doing?
Who is feeling the pain?
Who or what is driving the change?
When did the current state begin and when did it start causing pain?
Where is the bulk of the change likely to take place?
What new people, technologies, or processes are enabling the change?

Who can help?

Who should the stakeholders be?
Who should the change sponsor be?
Who wants to be part of the change?
Who can help to evangelize?
Who can help mitigate our risks?
Who will give us resources we need?
Who has the most to gain?

Change Planning Canvas™

Change Readiness (including Prerequisites)

What must be in place before you can begin?
What must be complete before you start?
How ready is the organizations for this change?

Risks and Negative Impacts

Any risk of lawsuits?
Any potential to lose key talent?
Will customers revolt?
Any chance expected benefits won't
be achieved?
Any chance we can't get the resources
needed to complete the change?

Mitigation Strategy

How can we decrease any legal risks?
How can we lock-in key talent through
the deployment period?
How can we quell any concerns that
customers may have about the change?
What actions can we take to secure the
resources we need, when we need
them?

Resources Controlled

What human resources do you have?
What capital do you have access to?
What materials do you have on hand?
What infrastructure is in place?
What intangible resources can you
leverage?

Resources Needed

What human resources do you need?
What capital do you need access to?
What materials do you need?
What infrastructure is needed?
What intangible resources do you need
access to?
How many people are change saturated
(involved with too many other change
effrts)?

Assumptions

Resource availability
Executive support
Timings
Customer wants and needs
What other assumptions are you
making?

Labor union work rules
Laws and regulations
Time of the year
Competing priorities
Potential misunderstandings
Trust level
Pre-requisites
Organizational politics
Budget

Barriers

Desired State, Vision, Change Target, and Critical Success Factors

Who are we making this change for?
Who will feel the greatest benefit from this change>
What is the solution that we'd like to see in place?
Why is this solution a big improvement over the status quo?
When do we need/want to complete the change process by? Is there a legal deadline?
Where will support come from for this change?
Where will the resources come from?
How does the vision for this change integrate with the company vision?
What are the critical success factors for this change? How will we measure whether the
change effort is a success?

Business Benefits

Will the change decrease costs?
Will the change increase revenue?
Will there be any process improvements?
Will fewer people be needed?
Will the change make things faster?

Figure P1.1 Change Planning Canvas™

Who will resist?

Who will feel threatened?
Will the change question competence?
Will the change cause layoffs?
Who will lose influence or power?
Will someone's budget be reduced?
Will someone have to do more work?

Who else is affected?

Who else feels pain?
Does the pain make the main sufferer reach out to others for help?
Will the change have impacts on other groups or individuals?

Change Phase 1 –Startup

What are the first actions to take to start moving from current state to desired state?
Who needs to be involved in this first phase?
What other resources are needed to successfully startup your change effort?
When does this phase need to be completed so the second change phase can begin?

Timeframe

Communication Series 1

What's the message?
Who is the target audience?
What communication channel will you use?
Why is this communication important?

Target Date

Change Phase 2 – Execution & Training

Do you see more than 10-20 steps remaining to reach the desired state?
(if YES then Change Phase 1 or 2 are too big and you'll need more than one canvas)
After the first set of actions in Phase 1 completes, what do you need to do next?
Who needs to be involved in this second phase?
What other resources are needed to complete this phase?
When does this phase need to be completed so the second change phase can begin?

Timeframe

Communication Series 2

What's the message?
Who is the target audience?
What communication channel will you use?
Why is this communication important?

Target Date

Change Phase 3 –Wrapup

Is this the final phase? Will you have reached the desired state after completing this step? (if NO then your phases are too big & need to be broken down onto additional canvases)

Who needs to be involved in this final phase?
What other resources are needed to complete this phase?
When does this phase need to be completed?

Timeframe

Communication Series 3

What's the message?
Who is the target audience?
What communication channel will you use?
Why is this communication important?

Target Date

Customer Benefits

Will the change improve the value proposition for customers?
Will the change allow for a lower price?
Will it improve customer service?
Will it get easier to do business with us?

Employee Benefits

Will the change improve retention?
Will it decrease turnaround times?
Will it increase processing speeds?
Will it make employees happier?

© BradenKelley.com

This book is designed to be an easy reference during your change planning process, and it comes with a handful of inspiring case studies and contributions from a set of guest experts sprinkled throughout the book. Taken together, the content that follows will serve as an excellent textbook for courses in organizational change or change management at universities, colleges, and vocational schools, and this book can serve as a guidebook for employees working in the change management, project management, and Agile Software Development professions.

On the web site www.charting-change.com you will find downloadable versions of select toolkit components designed to be printed on a variety of paper sizes, including:

- the Change Planning Canvas™ itself;
- a Visual Project Charter™ informed by the Project Management Institute's (PMI) project management body of knowledge (PMBOK) that can be used in your traditional project management efforts;
- a handful of Change Planning Toolkit™ components highlighted in the book;
- a visualization of the Association of Change Management Professionals' (ACMP) Standard for Change Management.

Many of the tools in the optional Change Planning Toolkit™ will look familiar to change management professionals because they have been informed by the ACMP's Standard for Change Management and the PMI's PMBOK.

Finally, it is no accident that you will find nearly interchangeable use of the terms *change initiative, change program, change effort*, and yes, even the term *project*. After all, what is a project but an effort designed by a group of people to change something about the organization (even a small thing)?

So, let's begin!

Acknowledgments

I want to thank first and foremost my wife, Kathy, for creating all of the great chapter page illustrations you'll see throughout the book and for giving me the confidence and support to pursue this project. I'd like to also thank my daughter Gabriella for contributing the whimsical final chapter page illustration.

When I finished writing my first book *Stoking Your Innovation Bonfire* back in 2010, I didn't think I'd ever write another book. But the past five years have reinforced the insight that the reason that most organizations are bad at innovation is that they are bad at change, and as I started investigating the reasons why, what kept jumping out is that change in most organizations is an overwhelming, inhuman process. I set out to find a way to help change this, and a solution came to me in a dream.

The Change Planning Canvas™ was born and the rest of the Change Planning Toolkit™ soon followed thanks to the feedback and support from Julie Anixter, Jason Rothstein, Lisa Oelsner, Gregory Paley, and others.

Everything about this book, from the chapter page illustrations to the toolkit itself, is designed to make change more accessible and more human and to blend its technical and artistic elements.

My work as an innovation keynote speaker, workshop leader, and co-founder of the world's most popular innovation web site, InnovationExcellence.com, has allowed me to attend a number of change management and innovation conferences around the country and to meet many really great people from around the world; my interactions with our community of 300+ contributing authors have helped evolve the research and thinking that have gone into this book.

I'd like to thank the great contributing authors you'll find in this book, including Matthew E May, Beth Montag-Schmaltz, Babak Forutanpour, Brett Clay, Ayelet Baron, Rohit Talwar, Seth Kahan, Ty Montague, Rosemarie Ryan, Tanveer Naseer, and Dion Hinchcliffe. I'd also like to thank the team at Britain's National Health Service (NHS) for contributing a great case study (including Helen Bevan, Kate Pound, and Rachel Timms).

I'd also like to thank my agent, John Willig, and my editor, Laurie Harting, for having faith in me and my concept and want to thank all the other people who worked behind the scenes at Palgrave Macmillan to help make this book a reality.

Finally, I'd like to thank the readers of my first book *Stoking Your Innovation Bonfire*. If it hadn't been for the sheer number of you who bought a copy of the book and the positive reaction I've received to the thinking contained in those pages, the inspiration to write another book may never have come. So, please keep reading, and who knows what might happen next.

BRADEN KELLEY

CHAPTER 1

Changing Change

"Does the change you're proposing inspire fear or curiosity? Fear steals energy from change; curiosity fuels it."—Braden Kelley

The Accelerating Pace of Change

The world is changing all around us at an increasing rate, and individuals (and organizations too) are struggling to cope with this ever increasing pace of change.

In fact, figure 1.1 highlights how over the past 50 years the average lifespan of a company on the S&P 500 has dropped from 61 years to 18 years (and is forecast to shrink further in the future).[1]

CompUSA and Circuit City used to be strong consumer electronics and computer retailers; now they're gone from the business landscape. Blockbuster Video used to dominate the video rental business; now it is a footnote in textbooks on disruptive innovation after being displaced by Redbox and Netflix. Kodak failed to transform its business to succeed in the digital age. Walmart and McDonald's both failed to change their business models and product offerings to suit the markets in Germany and Bolivia, respectively, and had to go out of business in those countries.

Technology is changing faster, and consumers are adopting new technologies faster than ever; consumer behaviors are shifting more quickly, and even political movements are happening with sudden swiftness. Remember the Arab Spring and how fast Egypt collapsed?

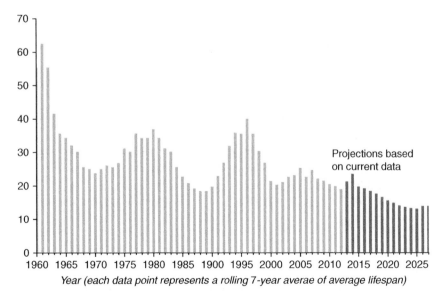

Figure 1.1 Average Company Lifespan on S&P Index in years (rolling 7-year average)

Source: Innosight/Richard Foster, "Creative Destruction Whips Through Corporate America," 2012.

It took nearly 90 years for the automobile to reach 90 percent of US households, but only 20 years for the mobile phone to reach that same milestone. The increasing pace of technology adoption by consumers leaves marketers feeling like they have an ever shrinking window of profit potential with each successive product launch.

While it is possible to enter a market too early, you can survive this tactical error if you enter in a small way instead of committing to a global launch with grand promises to customers. However, much more damage comes to organizations that enter too late. As leader of your organization, you must constantly strive to be faster at discovering new market insights and adapting and aligning your organization to fulfill newly discovered market needs more quickly than the competition; otherwise you might find your company locked out of your customers' set of primary considerations.

Avoiding Deadly Change Gaps

Of course, nobody wants to go out of business, but the fact is that your organization will likely have to change its sign from "Open" to "Closed," permanently, if it develops one or more of the following change gaps:

1. Your speed of internal change is slower than the rate of external change (including business, geopolitical, social, and economic changes in the world around you).
2. Your speed of innovation is slower than the competition's speed of innovation, including:
   a. market analysis (gathering of insights and inspiration)
   b. invention (creation of innovation source material)
   c. design (building a potential solution around an invention)
   d. development (taking the design and creating a scalable, launch-ready solution)
   e. test (evaluating with customers whether the solution works as designed and scales as intended)
   f. evolution (launching the solution into the marketplace with open eyes and ears, pivoting/improving as necessary)
3. Your resource flexibility (information, financial, physical, and human) is less than that required by the changes the organization faces.
4. Your hiring speed is slower than the speed of your growth.
5. Your speed of decision making is slower than what is required to keep up with the changes.

What other change gaps do you see as you look at your business or those of your competitors?

If companies are going to launch the products and services that consumers want, when they want them, managers are going to have to close any of the change gaps identified above that apply. Only then will they be able to maintain the rate of accelerated change necessary to survive in today's ultracompetitive marketplace. And if this is true for businesses, it is also true for nonprofit organizations and governments. The pace of societal change is accelerating. Just because an organization doesn't have a profit motive doesn't mean it doesn't have customers or that it can fail to exhibit the behaviors necessary to cope with continuous change.

The Need for Organizational Agility

In this new reality, organizations are going to need to change how they change, to increase their organizational agility, to increase the flexibility of the organization, to create a culture of continuous change and simultaneously inhibit the appearance and/or growth of the aforementioned change gaps.

One way to do handle these challenges is to take a more agile approach to change (see figure 1.2), to adopt some of the values and principles of the Agile Software Development methodology, and to use those to create a set of what could be described as agile behaviors within the organization. If you are not familiar with the Agile Software Development methodology, I have included below the Agile Software Development Manifesto from http://agilemanifesto. org that details the values and principles of Agile Software Development. As you read through the manifesto I hope you'll see that the values and principles can easily be applied to other endeavors outside of software development, whether to the project management discipline of your organization or to your larger change initiatives.

Manifesto for Agile Software Development[2]

We are uncovering better ways of developing software by doing it and helping others do it.

Through this work we have come to value:

- Individuals and interactions over processes and tools
- Working software over comprehensive documentation
- Customer collaboration over contract negotiation
- Responding to change over following a plan

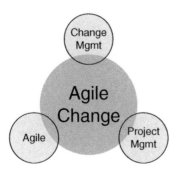

Figure 1.2   Agile Change

That is, while there is value in the items on the right, we value the items on the left more.

Principles behind the Agile Manifesto

We follow these principles:

1. Our highest priority is to satisfy the customer through early and continuous delivery of valuable software.
2. Welcome changing requirements, even late in development. Agile processes harness change for the customer's competitive advantage.
3. Deliver working software frequently, from a couple of weeks to a couple of months, with a preference to the shorter timescale.
4. Business people and developers must work together daily throughout the project.
5. Build projects around motivated individuals. Give them the environment and support they need and trust them to get the job done.
6. The most efficient and effective method of conveying information to and within a development team is face-to-face conversation.
7. Working software is the primary measure of progress.
8. Agile processes promote sustainable development. The sponsors, developers, and users should be able to maintain a constant pace indefinitely.
9. Continuous attention to technical excellence and good design enhances agility.
10. Simplicity—the art of maximizing the amount of work not done—is essential.
11. The best architectures, requirements, and designs emerge from self-organizing teams.
12. At regular intervals, the team reflects on how to become more effective, then tunes and adjusts its behavior accordingly.

You will see in figure 1.3 that constant change sits at the center, Agile Values providing the initial direction for an organization with a committed goal of becoming more agile. Radiating out from Agile Values as you pursue success

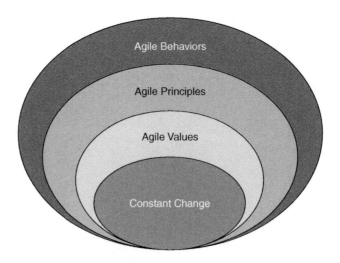

Figure 1.3   Agile Change Framework

in coping with constant change will be the Agile Principles. Ultimately you can't live the values or follow the principles if you don't exhibit behaviors that express those values and principles. Unless your organizations begin to behave in a more agile way, the potential of truly becoming more agile will go largely unfulfilled.

It is because of the challenge of behaving in a new way that I encourage you to make a move toward a formal pursuit of organizational agility. To help you in this pursuit, I will introduce elements of the Change Planning Toolkit™ in this book and make selected components available for download on the website www. charting-change.com.

Using this new set of tools and processes will not only make change seem less overwhelming, but it will also help you build alignment, get everyone on the same page for change, and create a more agile organization as adoption of the tools spreads.

Making Change Less Overwhelming and More Human

Change typically feels very cold and impersonal. Often when we think about change, it is something that we look at as being done to us, not something that we are part of.

Change frequently feels like a mechanical effort, not a human one. An effort often accompanied by a sense of dread as we recognize the need to start doing things differently. But given the anticipated number of moving parts, we're often unsure of where to begin. This typically leads to:

- an invasion of outside consultants;
- more work for the internal people charged with supporting the external consultants;
- a sense of unease and instability within the organization;
- the creation of reams of paper documents and hundreds of PowerPoint slides with pretty charts and graphs and tables that only mean something to a select few;
- the inevitable flood of emails, all-hands meetings, and mouse pads with cute slogans.

Change is overwhelming for most people, and this leads to inaction and preservation of the status quo until the pain of the status quo becomes too much to bear, or the promise of the change becomes so enticing that people are willing to drop their resistance and begin engaging in the activities necessary to realize the intended outcomes of the change. This dynamic is sometimes referred to as the burning platform,[3] and contrary to popular belief, Daryl Conner did not use the story to say that there must be an emergency before people will feel compelled to act. Instead, he likes to highlight four drivers relevant to the burning platform concept that can help shift people from inaction to resolute forward momentum. They include

1. current problems
2. current opportunities
3. anticipated problems
4. anticipated opportunities

What if change wasn't so scary and we could compel organizations to change in advance of any crisis? What if we could visualize the opportunities and benefits of change as vividly as people's understanding of the status quo? What if we could begin a change effort after identifying a promising idea, without encountering what is often a painful level of resistance? What if we didn't see change as intimidating because we feel empowered with an understanding of how change works? What if the rapid pace of change was part of the corporate culture, expected, and accompanied by a widespread feeling that it is possible to continuously change (unlearning and relearning as we go)? What if we were inspired by change instead of being scared by it because we believe the organization has the tools to help us successfully plan and execute a change to improve the organization or its potential for success?

Instead of imagining what all this might be like, we can live this ideal if we give people the tools and teach organizations how to use the tools to plan and execute change in a more collaborative, more visual, more kinetic, and more human way.

We must accelerate the trend of more kinetic and visual thinking in business, a trend started with tools such as mind mapping, graphic recording, and the business model canvas. Humans need to move, to discuss, to tell stories, to draw, and to contribute to the changes that will affect them and their subordinates and colleagues. When we all sit at our desks and type into our word processors, spreadsheets, and presentation tools, it is too easy to exclude others from the process and protect the status quo.

When we leave the safety of our cubicles, offices, and job descriptions behind and come together into a common space with a common language and a set of common tools to engage in a common dialogue about what changes are needed, how they will affect each individual, and how to best achieve them, then the walls come down and the uncommon becomes possible.

When we engage people's minds, bodies, and feelings then change becomes, well, more human.

Prototyping Change

There are many different trends, methodologies, movements, and ways of thinking that are converging at this moment in history to elevate and reinforce the role of the prototype in achieving everything from a successful startup to a blockbuster product launch.

These methods include design thinking, lean startup thinking, hack days, 3D printing, the maker movement, hacker culture, agile methodologies, and the minimum viable product (MVP). For those of you not familiar with design thinking, there are some highlights in figure 1.4.

The key concepts to remember about design thinking are:

- seeking to understand (empathizing often through observations and questions);
- defining the problem (or your point of view) in the right way;
- considering every possible solution before choosing one;
- prototyping your preferred solution, getting feedback, and repeating.

If it is a smart idea to prototype a new shopping cart or a new hospital room layout before building it, then why would it seem unreasonable that we should prototype our desired change in the same way?

The Change Planning Toolkit™ uses a collaborative, visual, and kinesthetic process I've developed to get people planning their change efforts in a new, more effective way. I will introduce the process and the visual elements throughout this book, giving your team a way of producing a mock-up what a potential change might look like. In the process you can identify some of the barriers you might face, capture the assumptions you're making at the outset, your view of what the future state might

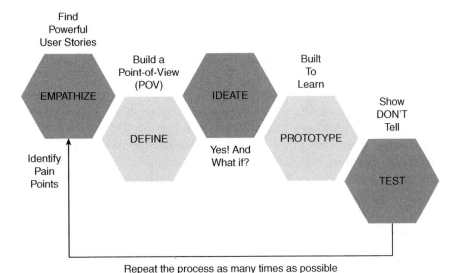

Figure 1.4 Design Thinking Cheat Sheet

Source: Guido Kovalskys and the Stanford University dSchool.

look like, among other things. We'll look at how to best investigate, discuss, agree, and document each change component as we progress through the book.

As you use my Change Planning Toolkit™ to kick off your next project or your next change initiative, keep thinking about what the minimum viable progress might be in order to maintain momentum. This is very similar to the idea of a minimum viable product, which is a key lean startup concept popularized by Eric Ries, author of the bestselling book, *The Lean Startup.*[4]

Minimum viable progress means that for projects and change initiatives to be successful, it is necessary to have a successful planning session where strong buy-in is achieved at the start, and it is equally important to show a level of progress sufficient to maintain the momentum and support for the project or change initiative you worked so hard to achieve at the start.

This is where those agile principles we highlighted earlier in the chapter come into play. The goal of our change or project planning efforts should be not just to prototype what the change might look like, but to also build a plan that breaks up the work into a cadence the organization can cope with and successfully implement into a new standard operating procedure. Many thought leaders extol the virtues of quick wins and that every project or change initiative should focus on them, but I believe structuring your project or change effort into a series of sprints will give you a sustainable flow of wins (and thus momentum) throughout the life of the project.

And in the end, momentum wins.

Creating Capability for Continuous Change

The accelerating pace of change and the increasing need for innovation to remain competitive calls for companies to shift the mindset of the entire organization to not only accept continuous change, but to embed it as a capability and competitive differentiator for the organization.

In the information technology area there is a big move underway as increasing numbers of software development organizations move from waterfall software development methodologies to embrace the agile method. But in the rest of the organization, most people still operate in a way that resembles the waterfall software development methodology, with each part of the organization doing its part and throwing its work over the wall for the next department to catch.

There are signs that this is changing, as some departments in an increasing number of organizations are looking at how they also can apply agile methodologies to their area, or apply lean thinking or design thinking or even lean startup thinking. The goal with all four of these methodologies is to focus more on value, customers, and experimentation. In the end, these methodologies lend themselves better to continuous change than our traditional ways of doing things, but they are not enough.

To truly create a capability for continuous change in organizations, we must help everyone understand the need for changing how we change and commit to doing things differently. We must look for the tools and processes our organizational culture is least likely to reject and adopt them at a speed that will limit organizational resistance to change.

We must seek to replace fear of change with curiosity about the new tools and processes that can help organizations achieve this new capability. We must then train as many people as possible in using the new tools and processes in order to replace that curiosity with understanding.

As people become more comfortable with new tools such as the Change Planning Toolkit™, participation in change efforts will become richer and more meaningful; people will begin to trust the processes more, and the speed of change in an organization will steadily increase.

Eventually, people will become so comfortable using the tools and working through the process that as they finish planning one change initiative or project, they will be ready to begin planning the next one, and with their experience and learning they will contribute to their organization's evolving overall change capacity. When this tipping point is achieved, the knowledge of the new change tools and processes will be easily disseminated throughout an organization by these new passionate champions. When this stage of evolution is reached the organization will have truly built the capability for continuous change.

Summary

We often think change is something being done to us, not something we are part of. Change is overwhelming for most people, and this leads to inaction and preservation of the status quo until the platform is truly burning.

But if companies are going to launch the products and services consumers want, when they want them, then companies must identify their change gaps and work to close them.

In this new reality we all face, organizations of all types are going to need to change how they change. One way to do this is to take more of an agile approach to change, to adopt some of the values and principles of the Agile Software Development methodology and use those to create a set of what could be described as agile behaviors within the organization.

To help you in this pursuit, we will introduce a collaborative, visual Change Planning Toolkit™ in detail in this book, and on the website www.charting-change.com you will find downloadable versions of select toolkit components.

We must accelerate the trend of more kinesthetic and visual thinking in business, a trend started with tools such as mind mapping, graphic recording, and the business model canvas. Humans need to move, to discuss, to tell stories, to draw, and to contribute to the changes that will affect them and their subordinates and colleagues. When we engage people's minds, bodies, and feelings then change becomes, well, more human.

Prototyping change is important too, and the Change Planning Toolkit™ gives you a way as a team to produce a mock-up of a potential change. It will also help you identify some of the barriers you might face, capture the assumptions you're making at the outset, and give you a view of what the future state might look like, among other things. To truly create capability for continuous change in our organizations, we must help everyone understand the need for changing how we change and commit to doing things differently and get people comfortable with this new set of tools.

CHAPTER 2

Planning Change

"What things will have to change for things to stay the same? What things will have to stay the same for things to change?"—Braden Kelley

Every bold action requires a plan if there is to be any hope of successfully achieving the intended outcomes. Planning helps people organize their thoughts and highlights the stakeholders and activities required to achieve a set of desired goals. Good planning shines a light on what might otherwise remain hidden. Planning aids in the refinement of objectives and the identification of integration points with other efforts underway in the organization. Good planning includes elements of forecasting and consideration of scenarios, aiding in the preparation of risk mitigation and other strategies necessary for reinforcing the chances of success. If you don't know where you are going, how will you know when you get there?

So What's Your Plan?

Change is everywhere; yet most organizations don't have anyone with the job title of change manager. You will find lots of project managers, program managers, product managers, Lean professionals, Six Sigma professionals, and an increasing number of people with business process management (BPM) and innovation titles, but you'll find very few people who were hired to fill a change management role. So how do people usually plan change?

Well, while you may not find many people in formal change management roles in organizations, you will find a plethora of change management and organizational change consultants. It's almost standard operating procedure in many companies to bring in a group of outside consultants when large-scale organizational change is needed, but the people with the other job titles mentioned above also regularly play a role in changing an organization, but their roles are often unaccounted for.

Failing to plan is planning to fail, and without a disciplined, repeatable easy-to-understand approach to change, the results are chaos and persistent resistance to change. The reality is that most organizations are failing to strengthen their capability to plan change in a consistent way, with a consistent toolset, and as a result, they are failing to grow the knowledge of how to productively plan and execute change. Because changing is not being practiced or trained, organizations do not become able to change faster as changes in their environment accelerate. In most organizations people plan change in an ad hoc way, everybody approaches it differently, and there is little gathering and sharing of best practices to improve change management knowledge and skills throughout the organization.

The Five Keys to Successful Change™

If we're hoping to change the world, whether big or small, we should begin by looking at the background of organizational change.

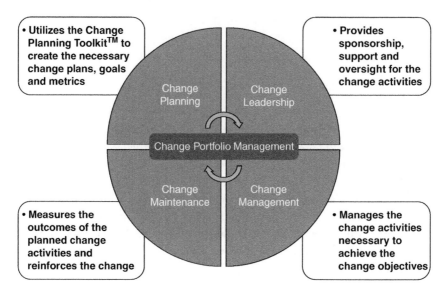

Figure 2.1   The Five Keys to Successful Change™

In figure 2.1 you see a visualization of The Five Keys to Successful Change™. Leave one out, and eventually your change effort will fail. If you're setting out to change the world, even a small corner of it, then you'll want to be sure to consider each of the five keys and make sure that you take each into account as you proceed.

Let's look at each of The Five Keys to Successful Change™ briefly before we look at each area in more detail throughout the book.

1. Change Planning
   • Change planning is the first key to successful organizational change, and it focuses on drawing out the key issues of the necessary change and puts them into a structure and timeline. You will find you have a better experience and a more successful outcome if you use a more visual, collaborative method—for example, using something like the Change Planning Toolkit™—to help you create the necessary change plans, goals, metrics, and so on.
2. Change Leadership
   • Change leadership is the second key to successful organizational change, and it is important because good change leadership provides the sponsorship, support, and oversight necessary for the change activities to receive the visibility and care so people can maintain momentum throughout the process of transformation.
3. Change Management
   • Change management represents the third key to successful organizational change, and it is probably the one most people think of when they think

about organizational change because it focuses on managing the change activities necessary to achieve the change objectives. The term itself, however, also refers to the management of code changes during the software development process, and therefore what differentiates it from project management is not always clear. We will examine the relationship between project management and change management in more depth later on.

4. Change Maintenance
   - Change maintenance represents the fourth and probably most neglected key to successful organizational change. Many change leaders lose interest after the major launch milestones are achieved, and this is a real risk to the change effort's sustained success. During the change maintenance phase the outcomes of the planned change activities should be measured and the change reinforced to make sure the change effort has met its objectives; this is also the time to make sure that the behavior change becomes a permanent one. If you neglect this phase, people often slip back into their old, well-worn patterns of behavior.

5. Change Portfolio Management
   - Every organization will have a broad collection of larger change efforts (digital transformation, merger integration, layoffs, etc.) and smaller change efforts (including all projects) underway or in the planning or maintenance stages at all times. This portfolio of change efforts must be managed and Change Portfolio Management represents the necessary activities for balancing all of the resource needs of this variety of change efforts.

Investing in Change

Almost nothing is scarier than being put in charge of a project and starting with a blank page in a plan that you are responsible for creating and managing. That overwhelming feeling becomes even stronger when that project is an organizational change initiative. But remember, ultimately every project changes something, and so if you want to be the leader of a successful project instead of an unsuccessful one, you must treat every project as a change initiative and aim not just for successful completion, but for willing participation and adoption.

For readers who have earned their Project Management Professional (PMP) certification from the Project Management Institute (PMI) and for readers who are not trained in the discipline of professional project management, I must reinforce that starting with a project charter is not enough. Professional project managers might argue that a project charter will provide the uniformity that is otherwise lacking in kicking off successful change efforts, or they might go in search of some similar Microsoft Word template that they think might do the trick. But the fact is that an approach focused on Microsoft Word documents in planning a change effort or project tends to be a solo activity, and nothing calls more for a collaborative approach than planning a change effort. If most organizations approach change planning in such an ad hoc fashion, with so many different people in the organization involved in many different ways (a woeful lack of consistency), then what is the solution?

The solution is to commit to making The Five Keys to Successful Change™ a capability of the organization and ultimately a competitive advantage. This requires investing in a common approach to change and a common set of tools for planning and executing it. Successful and sustainable change requires an investment in making one or more people the stewards of knowledge, tools, processes and best practices and training them to spread the tools and knowledge to others in the organization.

Understanding the Change Needed

Some of the first steps of planning any change effort are to identify what kind of change effort is being planned, who needs to be involved, and how to approach it. To help achieve some clarity in the initial murkiness of understanding what change approach is needed, I find it helpful to consider the intersection between the scope and type of change along with the leader's change leadership style and implementation strategy, which is pictured here in figure 2.2.

The following levels of change are fairly self-explanatory:

1. Multiple organizations
2. Entire organization
3. Business unit
4. Department
5. Work team
6. Individual

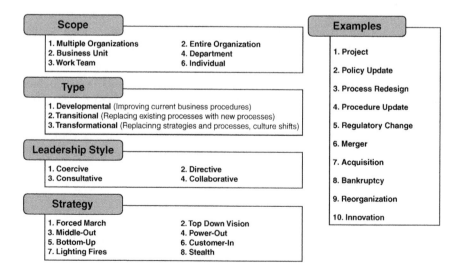

Figure 2.2   Determining the Change Approach

The scope of your change will give you an idea of what people you might want to invite to your change planning session(s).

The second major factor in your selection of change planning attendees will be the type of change. Here are some more details on the three major types of change identified by the government of Queensland:[1]

1. Developmental Change

   Developmental changes are those you make to improve current business procedures. As long as you keep your employees informed of changes and give them the training they need to implement process improvements, they should experience little stress from developmental change.

   Examples of developmental change include:
   - improving existing billing and reporting methods;
   - updating payroll procedures;
   - refocusing marketing strategies and advertising processes.

   Developmental change may be your first step to making further changes to your business that will help you meet the demands of your market. Managing these small steps well demonstrates to your team that you are taking a sensible, measured approach to change. When making developmental changes, it's important for you to:
   - explain to staff your rationale for the changes
   - train your staff to use new processes and technology
   - show your staff your commitment to minimizing the impacts of change on your business.

2. Transitional Change

   Transitional changes are those you make to replace existing processes with new ones. Transitional change is more challenging to implement and can increase your employees' discomfort.
   Examples of transitional change include:
   - experiencing corporate restructuring, mergers, or acquisitions
   - creating new products or services;
   - implementing new technology.

   The transitional phase of dismantling old systems and processes and implementing new ones can be unsettling for staff. When making transitional changes, you need to:
   - clearly communicate the impacts and benefits you foresee as a result of your changes;
   - reassure employees that their jobs are secure;
   - capture the views and contributions of your staff in making your changes
   - regularly update your employees on the steps you are taking to support them through the change and to train them in new systems.

3. Transformational Change

   Transformational changes are those you make to completely reshape your business strategy and processes, and they often result in a shift in work culture. These changes may be a response to extreme or unexpected market changes. Transformational change can produce fears and doubts in staff and needs to be carefully managed.

Examples of transformational change include:
- implementing major strategic and cultural changes;
- adopting radically different technologies;
- making significant operating changes to meet new supply and demand;
- reforming product and service offerings to meet unexpected competition and dramatic reductions in revenue.

Transformational changes usually involve both transitional and developmental change—where businesses recognize that they need to overhaul the way they do business. When making transitional changes, it's crucial that you:
- develop and communicate a well-defined strategy that explains the approaches you are taking to change and the goals you are setting;
- continually reinforce your rationale for the changes;
- plan and methodically implement new business systems and approaches;
- involve your staff in all phases of change discussions and planning and communicate regularly throughout the process.

The first two factors in the selection of change planning attendees were scope and and type, the third is leadership style. The change sponor must help identify the appropriate change leadership style for the change effort. Here are some more details on the four change leadership styles identified by David Straker:[2]

1. Collaborative

   A collaborative approach to change means involving the people affected, creating the change with them rather than doing the change to them. This works by pull people in and gaining commitment through getting them to invest in the change.

   A big dilemma with collaboration is the extent to which you allow people to make decisions rather than making recommendations about the change. Risks with giving away too much power include people making suboptimal, self-oriented choices or the devolved decisions across the organization not aligning with one another and hence creating more problems than they solve.

   A way of making collaboration successful is the what-how approach. In this method, the senior team still controls the strategic decisions and works out what needs doing. These priorities are then devolved to the rest of the organization—where more what-how deployments may occur.

   The problem with collaboration is that it takes time and effort, which relatively few organizations are willing or able to set aside. When speed is important, and resources are thin on the ground, then investing in collaborative efforts can seem wasteful.

2. Consultative

   A compromise to the completely collaborative approach is to show that at least you are listening to the people affected by the change. This may take the form of interactive real-time meetings, directors' tours, and so on. You can also use technology for web-enabled discussions and so on. You may also use suggestion schemes and the Request For Comment (RFC) approach, sending plans out to people for comment, but what you do with the comments received is entirely up to you.

   Care must be taken during consultation to ensure that people know the process and that they perceive it to be fair. As you move away from collaboration, greater trust is required of the decision makers and thus more trust-building activities may be required.

Consultative approaches provide a degree of balance between the engagement of collaboration and the push of direction and coercion.

3. Directive

    In a directive approach, there may still be a high level of communication, but it is now largely one-way. The organization is told how it will change. This is thus using the principle of push to drive through change. With the control of what happens in relatively few hands, the risk of variation in the plan is essentially removed.

    What will happen and when is laid out in a schedule that may or may not be publicized. The problem with this is leaders often fear that people will resist change more if they know what is going to happen. Resistance comes particularly from those who hold power (and it is surprising what power even the most junior person can have).

    To help reduce the problem of resistance, very high levels of communication may be required and a parental approach may be used ("father knows best" and "mother cares"). Thus, for example, generous severance packages may be offered to those who lose their jobs.

4. Coercive

    At the furthest extreme, a coercive approach pays little attention to the people, their ideas, or their needs. Changes are implemented in a relatively mechanical way.

    Typical of a coercive approach is the shock and surprise people encounter as change is thrust upon them. It is not unusual for people to arrive at work one Monday morning and find that they no longer have a job. Or they may be told that they are going to have to move far away across the country, a tactic sometimes used to reduce the workforce while complying with the law. Another variant is to bankrupt the company and then restart as a new company with all employees having to apply again for their jobs (this has been used to get around trade union issues).

    Not all coercive approaches are unethical, and some are simply born of the need for urgency. Ethics lie in the values of the people who are planning and implementing the change, rather than in the fact that a coercive approach is being used.

The fourth and final factor in your selection of participants for a change planning session is the change implementation strategy you select. Here are some more details on the eight change strategies identified by David Straker:[3]

1. Forced March

    Sometimes, though not often, the best approach is by simple command and control, telling everyone in the company exactly what to do.

    This may be essential in times of crisis (which may be manufactured in order to justify this approach) when there is no time for discussion, but otherwise it can result in significant resistance. This approach is only possible if the person in charge knows exactly what must be done.

2. Top-Down Vision

    This is the classic change pattern: The person or managing team at the top has a vision of the future and cascades this down through the organization.

A good way to do this is by a "what-how" cascade; at each step the senior person says, "This is what I want to happen." And the subordinate says, "This is how I can do it." This approach makes use of operational knowledge and helps promote buy-in.

A risk with this is that the sum of the actions at the front line of the organization does not add up to the original vision. It is also possible that operational realities make the vision impractical or unwise.

3. Middle-Out

In some organizations middle managers have a particular position of knowledge and influence. They are close enough to the front line that they understand operational realities and are also senior enough to have the trust of top management.

The principle here, then, is to put particular effort in engaging middle managers in defining and deploying the change. Other managers may still be involved, but the middle is given particular responsibility and authority to make the change happen.

4. Power-Out

Some organizations do not have a strong middle management, yet many have managers with distinct roles that include disproportionate power, such as factory managers and front-line supervisors. This strategy aims to find where power already exists and to focus efforts there to get buy-in and engage people in the details of making the change happen.

This approach has the advantage of "fishing where the fish are" in terms of using existing power structures rather than fighting the latter. This approach could still lead to a fragmented process with individuals thinking first of their own empire and only secondarily of the greater good.

5. Bottom-Up

In any company the people who are most hands-on and may well understand realities better than anyone else are the front-line people. Hence, you can start with these folks, engage them in discussions of how things are really working, and in this way seek to uncover opportunities and problems.

This may be swimming against the tide of managerial control, but this approach can be particularly effective when management is largely resisting the change. This approach can work with large workshops, putting front-line people on change committees, and rewarding individual initiative.

6. Customer-In

An effective way of creating an imperative to change is to start with customers and other key stakeholders. Do strong "listening" exercises, conduct surveys, and organize focus groups to understand your customers and what they like and dislike about you and your competitors.

Then focus all efforts on addressing these concerns. Keep the customer perception channel open throughout, maintaining conversations with representative customers and using surveys to provide a metric for showing improvements.

7. Lighting Fires

When you do not have consistent buy-in of managers, sometimes the only way is to try selling the idea for change. This is like lighting fires: some will go out, but others will catch and start making a difference. Then as you fan the flames, the fire gradually spreads.

This can be a slow process, and there is no guarantee of success, yet it is surprisingly common, particularly when there is no real buy-in from senior managers who may be taking a "wait and see" approach in order to avoid blame if things go wrong.

8. Stealth

An even more subtle way of creating change is to not tell anyone about it. Common ways of doing this include changing the policies that set organizational direction and the mechanisms by which people are motivated.

Catalytic mechanisms are levers that interlock to create change. For example, if you base bonuses on a customer satisfaction survey, then people will work to increase their bonus by making customers happy through improving service.

When initiating a change effort you must consider the intersections and individual influences of the following:

- scope of the change
- type of change
- appropriate change leadership style for the effort
- best choice of an implementation strategy

The end result will be that you'll have a clearer understanding of the change needed, the approach called for, and initial ideas for who to invite to the first planning session for your change or project. You will also now see potential power plays more clearly, because depending on the four factors for change above, some managers may begin to fight for their jobs or view the change as an opportunity to build new empires.

Who Needs To Be Involved?

Nothing is more important for creating successful change in an organization than getting the right people in the room and engaged during the change planning process. And if you want to get your change effort off to a strong start and set it up for success, then I encourage you to focus more on knowledge than on authority. Think about who knows the most about the key components of a holistic change plan. Take a moment to look at the Change Planning Canvas™ and consider which individuals in your organization will have the most knowledge and information. Also think about which individuals will provide the most considered viewpoints on the topics you will focus on as you work through the steps to create a fully populated Change Planning Canvas™ and then your execution plans.

The Eleven Change Roles™

Organizational change is a team sport, and in addition to attracting people with the relevant knowledge, information, and viewpoints to your change planning team, you must keep in mind The Five Keys to Successful Change™ and ensure that different roles are filled on the teams to drive success not only in change planning, but also in:

- change leadership (roles 10 and 11 are not needed here)
- change management (role 11 is not needed here)
- change maintenance (role 11 is not needed here)

My research into identifying the roles required to build successful change and transformation teams led to the creation of The Eleven Change Roles™ as a way of helping organizations build more complete and effective change teams. The Eleven Change Roles™ highlighted in figure 2.3 are comprised of:

1. Authority Figures/Sponsors

Somebody has to be in charge. This includes one main sponsor and a coalition of authority figures that can help push things forward when a push is required.

2. Designers

Designers are your big picture thinkers, people who can see how the pieces fit together; they are skilled meeting facilitators, know the methodology well, and can help keep people on track as you build the plans for your change effort.

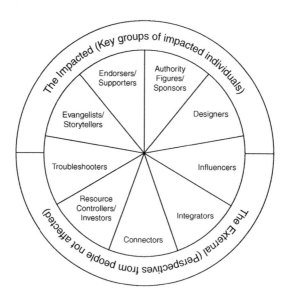

Figure 2.3 The Eleven Change Roles™

3. Influencers

Influencers are well-respected and forceful people in the organization. They may lack the formal position power of a sponsor or authority figure, but they can help rally people to the cause with their words and actions.

4. Integrators

Integrators are good at bridging silos, building relationships that cut across geographies and hierarchies, and finding ways for different work teams and departments to work together to achieve a common goal.

5. Connectors

Connectors are slightly different from Integrators in that they know where the overt and hidden resources lie in the organization; they have the personal connections and influence necessary to open a dialogue that can result in a needed connection.

6. Resource Controllers/Investors

These people have things you need—human resources, information resources, and physical resources. You must get them to invest those resources to successfully achieve your desired change.

7. Troubleshooters

There are always going to be problems along the way, some expected and some not. Troubleshooters are really good at helping identify those problems and they enjoy the challenge of finding ways around, over, under or through these potential barriers when they crop up. It is even better when the team can identify ways to overcome the problems before communications to the rest of the organization begin. Troubleshooters can help with this and often have the domain knowledge or the insight into the change target's mind-set necessary to move minds and resources to support the change program.

8. Evangelists/Storytellers

About every change effort a story can be told describing the desired future state as better than the current state and worth the disruption of making the change. The story builds a vision, creates themes that will weave together into the story, and symbols that will reinforce and show your commitment to realizing the goals you set for the change effort. Without this evangelism and storytelling it will be hard for people to understand what you are trying to do or to support it.

9. Endorsers/Supporters

Getting people to agree to talk up the change effort even if they are not taking an active role in pushing it toward completion is very powerful. Don't be afraid to reach out and ask for this seemingly insignificant assistance, but arm these individuals with the themes, symbols, and stories that will reinforce the vision and sustain momentum.

10. The Impacted (key groups of impacted individuals)

Who's going to be affected by this change? Don't be afraid to invite these people early on to voice their concerns so that you can understand their objections, identify solutions or mitigations, and potentially recruit them as effective evangelists.

11. The External (perspectives from people not affected)

It's easy to miss risks, assumptions, barriers, and points of potential resistance when you are too close to the effort. Inviting in some people from outside your organization to be part of your planning process or getting their feedback on what you are trying to do will be enlightening because they have a fresh, detached perspective.

When you take the time to thoughtfully recruit people into all of The Eleven Change Roles™ listed above, you will have a rich set of inputs, a lively discussion, and a strong set of outputs from your change planning process. Getting the right people with the relevant knowledge in the room and engaged during the change planning process will get you off to a strong start and set your change effort up for success. Having people with a strong ability to verbalize meaningful, well-intentioned, and well-informed contributions regarding the key components of the Change Planning Canvas™, will provide you with powerful content as you populate your execution plans.

Change Planning Team Contributions

Creating a change planning team that can bring the information and influence to the table that you really need is one of the keys to the eventual success of your change planning sessions and the overall change effort as a whole. The information you need will obviously be driven by the topics that your team should cover as part of your change planning efforts. These include:

- What is the current state?
- What are the change drivers? (It is helpful to discuss history, context, and the main proponents.)
- Is there a budget for both planning and executing this change?
- What other change programs are in progress or about to begin?
- How ready are we as an organization to make this change?

- What must we know, what must we have, what must we complete before we begin?
- What does the desired state look like, and who are we targeting with this change?
- What is our vision for moving from the current state to the desired state?
- Who can help us achieve this change?
- Who is most likely to resist this change?
- Who else is affected by this change aside from the change target?
- What are some of the risks and potential negative impacts of this change?
  ○ Who is affected? How? What are our mitigation strategies?
- What necessary resources do we already control? What other resources will be needed?
- Where does change saturation exist?
- What are some of our assumptions as we plan this change effort?
- What barriers (logistical, financial, etc.) are we likely to encounter as we move forward?
- What are the expected benefits (for the business, customers, and employees) of the change?
- What change phases (start-up, training, etc.) will we need to have for the change effort?
- What different series of communications, symbols, and signals will be helpful to the effort?
- How will we measure success (goals, metrics, critical success factors, progress, and momentum measures)?

We will dig into all of these questions in greater details in the chapters that follow by highlighting methodologies, processes, and frameworks that deepen engagement with each topic, and we will bring in selected tools from the Change Planning Toolkit™. In between chapters of this book you will find a small number of hand-picked case studies and commentary from guest experts focusing on additional best practices and next practices. All of these things together will help you get a better grasp on how to build your Change Planning Canvas™ effectively during your change planning kickoff event with your chosen team.

Starting the Change Planning Process

Planning a change effort can be an uncomfortable and overwhelming undertaking for just about anyone, but it doesn't have to be. Nearly a third of change efforts begin with no planning at all. Some managers succumb to the temptation of sitting down in front of a blank project chart or change management template in Microsoft Word and think it is easiest to plan the whole change initiative by themselves. This is obviously dangerous, and for most of us facing a blank Microsoft Word template is a scary prospect. This is no way to begin a change effort.

So far, we've laid the foundation for a commonsense approach to collaboratively and visually planning your change effort using the Change Planning Toolkit™. As you familiarize yourself with the toolkit's components, the kit will feel familiar and comfortable because the approach is based on people's behaviors and motivations and is based on the Project Management Body of Knowledge (PMBOK) principles of the Project Management Institute (PMI) and on principles from the Association of Change Management Professionals' (ACMP) Standard for Change as well as on best practices from a number of different sources. Some new approaches destined to become next practices are also included here.

Step One: Creating a Cozy Home for Change

First you will want to secure a room you can have for at least three days and that has at least one big blank wall. The reason is that you want to be able to download all of the elements of the Change Planning Toolkit™, print them as large as you can (especially the Change Planning Canvas™), and then put up those printouts on that blank wall. You should place the canvas at the center and the various worksheets around it.

You'll want to place the first half of the worksheets to the left of the Change Planning Canvas™ and the second half of the worksheets to the right. There is a logical order here, and figure 2.4 highlights the recommended layout. All worksheets are numbered in the Change Planning Toolkit™ to help you match the layout. Be sure and print out several communications worksheets and layer them.

This setup will give you plenty of space to capture all of the relevant information as you proceed through your change planning day, and it will also help guide people's thinking and expectations so that they are prepared to provide the appropriate information at the right time.

The room should be fairly empty. I would recommend having a small table with supplies (pens, markers, sticky notes, etc.) in one back corner of the room and another small table in the other back corner of the room with beverages and snacks. You will probably also want to have a few small round tables with chairs for people to sit down and write on sticky notes, but primarily you want people to be on their feet and add their notes and insights to the Change Planning Wall; they should be talking about their contributions instead of sitting passively.

I would also encourage you to cover the other walls of the room with photographs, drawings, and other props that will serve as reminders of what the current state looks like as well as with other images and objects that will serve as inspiration for what the desired state might look like.

Step Two: Familiarize Your Team with the Change Planning Toolkit Process and Tools

The second step in preparing to hold a change planning session is to refamiliarize yourself with the various elements of the toolkit and its central component, the Change

Planning Canvas™. Think about how you would explain these items to others. Next you will want to organize a session before the actual change planning session to familiarize your participants with the elements of the toolkit and your way of using them.

You should plan on spending day 1 of 3 on setting up the room and setting the stage and familiarizing your team with the process and tools you will use during your change planning session (big changes or transformations may require an extra day).This may seem redundant or you may worry that as you explain the elements of the toolkit or as people see the Change Planning Canvas™ they may sidetrack you and try to jump into providing content for the worksheets or the canvas itself.

The solution is to hand everyone a small notebook at the beginning of the session and instruct your participants that this notebook is to capture any pieces of inspired thought they may have as you explain how the Change Planning Canvas™ and the rest of the toolkit will be used. Explain that each page has been labeled with the topic the worksheets will cover and that you will describe how each of the worksheets (and the canvas) will be used so that it is easy for people to capture ideas and comments both during the session and when they are back at their desks (or even at home).

As a result, you will get through all worksheets and the canvas and focus this training session on making sure that everyone understands the process and the tools and their use. In this forum people have the opportunity to ask questions until they understand the process and the tools before starting the planning session proper. Moreover, people can write down their ideas in their notebook and come to your change planning session armed with information and ideas to contribute to the conversation at the appropriate time.

Step Three: Setting the Stage

You can't begin any change planning session without first providing an orientation for people on what the agenda for the session is, what your goals are for the event, and what the expected outcomes are. That is, you must let people know where they can find supplies or tools they might need (pens, sticky notes, etc.), what refreshments and meals are available (and when), and so on.

Then you will want to tell people a story. The story that you are going to tell people is about the reasons for the images and objects that you've chosen to place around the room and on the tables. You'll want to explain that the two things people will always want to keep in mind are the current state and the desired state. Then you'll want to remind everyone that what you need most are their thinking and their participation; explain that the strength of the plans that will result from the session's activities—and ultimately the success of the change effort—will depend on the level of honesty, participation, collaboration, and dialogue created during that session.

Step Four: Light the Fire and Have Fun!

The reason that we are planning change this way is to humanize the process and make it less overwhelming and more fun.

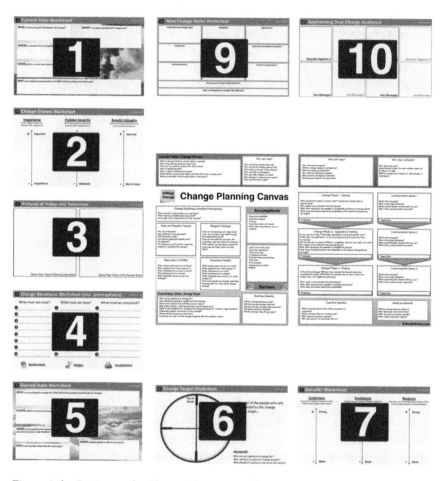

Figure 2.4 Setting up the Change Planning Wall

Resources and Change Saturation Worksheet

Barriers Worksheet — Strategies to Overcome

Risks Worksheet — Mitigation Strategies

Change Phases Worksheet

Change Phase 1 - Start

Change Phase 3 - Wrapup

Negative Impacts Worksheet

Who is Affected | How Are They Affected* | Mitigation Strategies

Change Ripple Worksheet

People Worksheet

Who can HELP?

Who else is AFFECTED?

Communication Series #1 Worksheet

Why is this communication important?

Who is the target audience?

What communication channel will you use?

As for any off-site or workshop, you will want to plan on doing some icebreaker exercises at the beginning to help people get to know each other and relax. Unless your organization is fairly small, your participants may not all know each other.

One good icebreaker to get people in the mood for a session of change planning is to have people write on note cards two change efforts they were a part of (one that succeeded and one that failed). Ask them to also note what they thought were the reasons for the success or failure of those change efforts. Then have people mingle and trade their cards away. Consider requiring people to gather two or three check marks on each card before they can trade their cards so that they must have more than two conversations. Require people (if possible) to have conversations only with those they didn't know before.

You should plan on spending two days (or possibly more for big changes) on these activities because planning a change is complex and because you want to allow time for the dialogue likely to result as you work through the process (which is key to building buy-in, ownership, and accountability).

Two whole days is a long time for people to spend away from their jobs, so I would recommend scheduling the days so that people have time to address the inevitable urgent matters at the beginning or end of the day or during a longer break in the middle of the day. However, change is urgent too, and you need everyone present and participating for the necessary dialogue and alignment to occur. You must also have a very strict policy about not having phones or laptops in the room. Consider having people place these gadgets in a box by the door at the beginning of the session.

To maintain the energy and focus required for good insights and good participation, you should plan a short break every 60 or 90 minutes. Consider ringing a bell and having everyone change chairs whenever you notice people's energy starting to flag. I would encourage you to have some other activities planned that involve movement and some shots of inspiration ready to boost the enthusiasm in the room if people start to get quiet.

Keep in mind that just because you have 30 minutes scheduled for a particular topic you do not have to use that time all at once. Move on when discussion stalls and look for graceful opportunities to lead people back to unfinished discussions to add more information on the topics people were not ready to discuss completely earlier. To humanize the process, you must watch for nonverbal cues and let the process find its own pace so it feels less forced and more natural.

Finally, every group is different and every project or change initiative is unique, and you may start out thinking that two days is a long time and then find it's not enough time. You need to have a contingency plan for that eventuality. At other times you might think you will not be able to guide a particular group through the topics and process in two days but find that you get through everything in much less time.

The key is to work through all of the topics in a meaningful, honest, and detailed way and have clear and concrete plans for executing what you capture on your Change Planning Canvas™. And every time you do this, the experience will be different. You'll learn something as a facilitator, and the participants will become more confident about using the processes and tools for their future projects and change initiatives. As a result, the methodology will spread to others and make successful changes possible throughout your organization.

Just don't forget to have fun! So let's summarize and then begin.

Summary

Planning your change process is a way to take control of the journey from your current state to the desired state at the end of your change effort. A plan based on my Change Planning Toolkit™ and the approaches detailed in this book will give you a chance of becoming one of the only 30 percent of change efforts that meet their stated goals.

Convincing your organization to invest in the tools and processes necessary to drive success in achieving change is the first step in your change planning journey. The next is to expand that commitment to include making The Five Keys to Successful Change™ a capability of the organization, and ultimately a competitive advantage. This means investing in one or more people to be the stewards of your knowledge, tools, processes, and organizational change best practices and spreading the tools and knowledge to other parts of the organization.

With a committed organization behind you, you can then look at the first change effort you will tackle using the new tools and processes detailed in this book. This includes understanding the change you are dealing with and the best way to approach it, encompassing identification of the scope, type, leadership style and strategy that are most appropriate given the different variables.

With a good understanding of the change you have chosen, you can then identify the people who you want to be involved in your change planning efforts. You can also choose the people who will be best suited to helping you execute your change plans.

Selecting the right people to participate in your change effort, people who bring the relevant information to a carefully constructed change planning event, is your key to initiating forward momentum for change in the execution of plans that will move you toward your desired state and expected outcomes.

CHAPTER 3

Understanding the Current State

"Sometimes we focus on the door that has just closed, and miss the door that just opened."—Braden Kelley

The Status Quo

Whether we want to admit it or not, there is a benefit to everything we do. This is why a pattern of behavior becomes the status quo. There is a benefit for continuing the behavior. But there is always some kind of pain, discomfort, or inconvenience involved with making a change. Sometimes we call the reluctance to change inertia or in the case of companies, charities and governments we call it organizational inertia. Often the status quo is benign, and this organizational inertia is harmless. But situations also arise where our inertia deprives us of receiving a greater benefit.

In many situations we fight to maintain the status quo to our detriment. This behavior is probably most obvious when we look at alcoholics, smokers, companies going out of business, and political administrations in trouble. From the outside we quickly realize that they continue to indulge in their destructive behavior, and most of us on the outside shake our heads and fail to understand why. In fact, sometimes the negative behavior not only continues as everything disintegrates, it intensifies. Why do individuals and companies fight so hard to maintain a status quo that is delivering fewer benefits than another potential future? The reason is that humans in a state of inertia, even when they *see* the potential benefits of a change, *feel* only the pain.

"An object at rest tends to stay at rest, and an object in motion tends to stay in motion."
—Isaac Newton

Sharpening the Axe

As you look to begin your change effort (or even your project), remember these words of Abraham Lincoln: "Give me six hours to chop down a tree, and I will spend the first four sharpening the axe."

Sharpening the axe in this case involves standing in the current state and looking back to understand:

- Who benefits from the status quo and how?
  - Who has the power?
  - Who has the knowledge?
  - Who has the expertise?
  - Who has a job as a result?
  - Are government agencies involved?

- What are the benefits of maintaining the status quo?
  - business benefits
  - customer benefits
  - employee benefits
  - government benefits
- Have people tried to change the status quo before?
  - How?
  - What were the results?
  - Is anyone still around who was involved with that effort?

After standing in the current state and looking back, you will then want to keep your mind on the current state and turn your eyes forward and examine:

- Why change now?
  - The status quo was acceptable for a while. Why is it now unacceptable?
  - What are the change drivers?
- What are the elements of context surrounding the change?
  - economic environment
  - organizational psychology
  - regulatory environment
  - competitive environment
- Who are the main proponents of this change?
  - Are they the same people feeling the bulk of the pain?
- Where is the bulk of the change likely to take place?
- What will happen if we don't change?
- Is there a budget for both planning and executing the change?

Picturing the Current State

One of the worksheets you'll find in the toolkit is titled "Pictures of Today and Tomorrow" (see figure 3.1). It is often helpful to have the people involved draw a picture of what the current state looks like to them.

This simple act can sometimes ignite people's creativity, but it also helps those who are more visually oriented to explain their thoughts better than they can by using only words. Use this exercise as a source of inspiration for your communication efforts (possibly unlocking signals, symbols, and themes) about the change you are planning.

Through the Looking Glass (Advocating that We DON'T Change)

To build upon the exercise of picturing the current state, pass out poster boards to those attending your change planning sessions and have them make a poster championing the status quo. This will help you and your team examine the status quo and the inertia you'll have to overcome to make the change process a success.

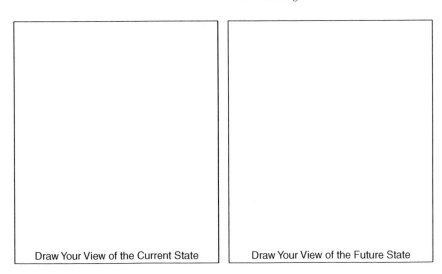

Figure 3.1 Pictures of Today and Tomorrow

As you prepare for the first day of your change planning session, ask everyone to bring some old magazines and catalogs. After participants have finished making their posters in the 10 to 15 minutes you give them, select a few volunteers to present their posters as if they were in a high school debate. Next guide a short conversation about what we can learn from looking at the opposite side of the change debate, and then tape all of the posters on a wall.

Capturing the Current State in Words

After drawing pictures of today and tomorrow and advocating against the change, participants should be better equipped to describe the current state in detail. One way to capture the specifics of the status quo is to leverage the Current State Worksheet from the toolkit that focuses on the following themes:

- who
- what
- when
- where
- why

In the section "Sharpening the Axe" above you'll find several guiding questions to start a dialogue about each of the above words.

Understanding the Change Drivers

The final step in effectively and completely understanding and capturing the current state involves switching from looking back and inward to looking forward and outward, focusing on evaluating the change drivers on a number of different dimensions. The intent is to provide greater visibility and group understanding of the change drivers for your project or initiative. Get the group to build a list of change drivers and rank each of them based on:

1. their relative importance
2. level of problem severity
3. level of benefit criticality

One way to organize this information is to utilize the Change Drivers Worksheet from the toolkit. Ranking the relative importance of various change components along with the relative severity of the problem and importance of the benefit will help the group see which levers are the most critical for the group to work on.

Summary

In this chapter we looked at a variety of tools at our disposal from the Change Planning Toolkit™ to help us better understand the current state and the change drivers (along with some other visual, auditory, and kinesthetic techniques). The key to understanding the current state is to understand why the status quo is dominant. Only after investigating the status quo and where its benefits and pain points come from can you understand the change drivers and see what the path toward achieving alignment of the organization around the change might look like. Our investigation of the current state also included standing in the current state and looking both back and forward to understand the context of the status quo and think about how we might help people see and feel the benefits of the change we are planning to make.

NHS Case Study

Challenge Top-Down Change (@NHSEngland, @HSJnews and @NursingTimes)

NHS Improving Quality, a national improvement body of NHS England, working in partnership with the Health Service Journal (HSJ) and the Nursing Times (NT) national healthcare management titles collaborated to challenge top-down change in the public health system.

www.hsj.co.uk/leadership/change-challenge

Challenging Top-Down Change

Background

The English National Health Service (NHS) was established in 1948 to deliver free health care to those who live in the United Kingdom. The NHS employs over 1.2 million full-time staff and is considered one of the largest employers in the United Kingdom and the fifth biggest employer globally. Since its establishment it has gone through many changes. Many of the changes in the NHS have been seen as very top-down via central government or senior management in the organization; however, it has not always been welcome by those directly affected by these changes. There is now recognition that change is changing, and therefore our approach to leading change in large organizations needs to be different (Hamel 2014; Gbadamosi 2015a).

The "Change Challenge" project was an experimental design to establish how we could deliver change led from the edges of the NHS. This was the first countrywide experiment to build a platform to capture the "wisdom of the crowd" and offering access to all to get involved. The project objective was to test the possibilities and capabilities of new methodologies discussed in the white paper "The New Era of Thinking and Practice in Change and Transformation" (Bevan and Fairman 2014), specifically crowdsourcing, to engage wider audiences to harvest ideas and insights. The project was also to test how the NHS can challenge the culture of top-down (driven by senior management) change. The project was delivered through a partnership working within NHS Improving Quality, a national improvement body of NHS England, the *Health Service Journal* (HSJ) and the *Nursing Times* (NT) national health care management publications.

The aims of the project were to:

- engage a wider audience with new methodology for large-scale change in a health care setting;
- build on new thinking and practice regarding theories of change;
- test out what is possible and push the boundaries using new-era methods of open social innovation in health care;
- curate and publish examples of open and social innovations that have been applied in health care and other industries, learning from others' experiences and drawing conclusions from lessons learned;
- produce "how-to" guides and build a "new-era" strategy to disseminate and share the learning.

Our Methodology

The Change Challenge used a methodology developed by the behavior change and crowdsourcing agency Clever Together. Similar to the problem solving approach some call "hackathon" or "sprints." the partnership ran four phases of crowdsourcing activity over 10 weeks (Clever Together 2015). Throughout the project engagement of the community was seen as key because without that there would be no crowd to engage with. *HSJ* and the *Nursing Times* published weekly articles and blogs on the subject area and kept a high social media presences via Twitter and Facebook.

Phase 1: Understand the Problem We Have to Solve

The crowd was invited via direct email, social media, and the *HSJ* and *Nursing Times* online magazines to participate on the platform to answer the question: "What things help or block you when you try to create bottom-up change?" This phase focused on creating discussion on the subjects and inviting people to be involved. Supporting articles and blogs were published in both the *Nursing Times* and the *HSJ* to engage and inform people on the subject matter.

Simple steps to start crowdsourcing for solutions (Clever Together 2014) are the following:

1. agree on objectives of the session
2. define challenge questions
   a. understand the scope of the challenge and design challenge questions to pose to your crowd
3. set up and seed platform
   a. input challenge questions onto the platform
   b. "seed" the platform with answers to the challenge question—ideas/plans/projects:
      i. existing
      ii. potential

       iii. realistic

       iv. radical

4. invite your "crowd" to solve the challenge
   a. tell your people/networks about the challenge, get them interested, and invite them to help
5. empower your crowd to share and build insights/solutions
   a. give your crowd the tools to share, elaborate, and prioritize ideas
   b. ensure leaders have the process to keep the conversation active and on track
6. start getting input from the crowd

The online platform was open for two weeks. People were asked to submit their thoughts on what helps or prevents bottom-up change within the NHS. Participants were also offered the opportunity to comment and vote on other people's suggestions. At the end of this two-week phase the platform was closed and content analyzed. The analysis identified what the crowd considered were the barriers and building blocks to bottom-up change (Thomond 2015).

Phase 2: Seeking the Answer

The second phase considered what the solutions to the problems are. The barriers and building blocks identified in phase 1 were presented to the crowd who were then asked to use this new knowledge to develop ideas on how we could create bottom-up change. Examples of solutions that are already in place were also requested so that successful methods could be developed as part of the hack. In this phase the members of the crowd were invited to input their ideas and thoughts on the online platform and to add comments on other suggestions and to vote.

At the end of this two-week period content analysis took place that drew on the wisdom of the crowd as to what they thought would work to deliver bottom-up change. Seven solutions were identified, and we moved into phase 3 of the hack.

Phase 3: Sensing and Prioritizing the Solutions from the Crowd

This phase focused on building the 47 solutions with the crowd. At this stage people were asked to input their suggestions on how the final solutions could be developed. Again people were able to input their thoughts on the platform and vote on the solutions they liked or thought would work in practice.

This phase also ran for two weeks. At the end of this period the final content analysis was completed; it identified the 16 final solutions.

Phase 4: Act and Share

This phase allowed time for the design team to work with the individuals and groups whose ideas had been selected to be elaborated into workable solutions that others could then test out. Working with the teams at the *HSJ* and the *Nursing Times*, the project members then published all the final solutions in the interactive online guide.

The result is a cutting-edge interactive guide that can inspire staff at every level to overcome the barriers to bottom-up change and to create the conditions that support this critical process within the United Kingdom's health economy (Health Services Journal 2015).

The Results

A total of 3,595 people from 45 different countries, contributed 13,895 ideas, comments, and votes. Of the participants surveyed before and after the project, we found nurses were the largest group, making up 33 percent of the total, followed by 12 percent allied health professionals, 8 percent doctors, 6 percent improvement leaders, and 6 percent business leaders. The results were categorized into the three groups shown in figure 3.1.1 and described below.

The final barriers to bottom-up change and the narrative behind them are listed below:[1]

1. Confusing Strategies

Our organizational strategies hold us back; they fail to provide a clear "call to action" to change things from the bottom up. They reinforce inflexibility in our business structures as well as leadership that is controlling.

Often there are so many priorities that it isn't clear to people what they should do. This leaves people fearful of stepping up and without the autonomy to deliver change effectively.

2. Overcontrolling Leadership

Despite some efforts, we inthe NHS still rely on command-and-control leadership rather than on coaching and nurturing. We perceive that we do not have the freedom or trust to create change from the bottom up.

Figure 3.1.1 NHS Top-Down Change Challenge

It's not that our leaders are bad—they just do not have the right skills. This leaves many employees feeling afraid of speaking up, which restricts bottom-up change.

3. One-way Communication

Often our leaders communicate at us rather than with us. We in the NHS are not open and transparent with each other.

We also do not have enough formal/informal ways of connecting creative people. One reason for this is a lack of soft skills training and technical systems to support communication.

4. Poor Workforce Planning

It feels like we either don't have enough people or enough time to get involved in driving change from the bottom up. One reason for this is that we often don't have the right mix of skills in our teams. We have a skills deficit because we are failing to nurture our people and organize the right mix of talent.

To get the right number of people with the right skills requires us to work in partnership with organizations other than our own—something we are not very good at.

5. Stifling Innovation

There is no shortage of ideas among health care staff. The challenge is a shortage of processes to capture ideas and a lack of leaders who truly empathize with the needs that we see here in the NHS. Senior leaders are trapped in inflexible processes. And we as an organization fail to embrace ways of taking part in low-cost, low-risk experiments to test ideas. We must utilize the diverse experiences of stakeholders, including our patients.

6. Playing It Safe

Our hierarchical, centralized structures either make it too difficult to access funding and support for ideas, or we end up funding too many projects with not enough resources. It seems that a lack of clarity on what's needed from leaders, plus a fear of doing something new from the bottom up, leaves us supporting the usual low-risk ideas.

7. Poor Project Management

When developing and implementing projects, we tend to value inputs and action rather than value and outcomes; this means as an organization we're kept busy, with no room for effective bottom-up change.

We underestimate the complexity in which we are working, and we blame inflexible processes and lack of resources. However, when change is led from the top and explained to all and we are trained to manage and implement projects, this process ultimately undermines bottom-up change too.

8. Undervaluing Staff

For the NHS to have a positive mind-set and ultimately ensure the well-being of our people, we need to treat each other with compassion, much as we would treat our patients. Alas, we don't always do this.

All too often we do not feel connected to our organization's purpose and do not feel that we have a real stake in its future. Feeling like a cog in the engine, rather than a value-adding individual, makes us feel undervalued, disengaged, and even ill. Why would we proactively get involved in change?

9. Inhibiting Environment

Our physical environment can keep us from meeting people and connecting ideas. The closure of various health care facilities has put a burden on the remaining organizations. And as we all know, our IT systems do not help us access knowledge and share information.

10. Perverse Incentives

The incentive system and performance management regime creates disincentives for bright ideas that might create better outcomes for patients but might increase operating costs. The existing system creates incentives that leave us stuck supporting self-serving projects

The building blocks to bottom-up change defined by the crowd are listed below along with the narratives behind them:[2]

1. Inspiring and Supportive Leadership

Leaders need to inspire and support their people. This means taking up ideas to improve organizations based upon the quality of the ideas rather than their author; a less hierarchical structure, where people have a greater understanding of each other's roles; and "distributed leadership," where people are trusted and talent is nurtured.

2. Collaborative Working

Collaboration between peers within and between organizations leads to broader operational and personal benefits. Operationally, change programs are more effective, allowing us to improve the outcomes for people and populations, and collaborative working builds more supportive working relationships, which is essential to improve people's well-being.

Peer collaboration therefore nurtures a more positive mind-set and the desire and connections to drive bottom-up change.

3. Flexibility and Adaptability

To deliver bottom-up change, we need flexibility in the system—both in the formal organizational structure and the day-to-day processes. This will allow organizations, teams, and individuals to adapt successfully to the changing environment in which they are operating.

4. Smart Use of Resources

We must try to find ways of doing more with the resources we have. The world's most successful organizations are more resourceful than their competitors. By adopting a resourceful mind-set and providing appropriate staffing and the right skill mix, we can try to deliver change within our current means.

We should aim for smarter project selection: doing the right projects well, rather than trying to do too much with not enough resources.

5. Autonomy and Trust

Increasing people's sense of trust gives them the confidence and permission to deliver change. This makes the most of the knowledge and passion of people working in health care.

We need to work within acceptable clinical parameters, remove the fear associated with failure, and foster a no-blame culture of reflection on what works and what does not.

6. Challenging the Status Quo

Everyone is able to create and identify great ideas; organizations need to nurture and embrace the creativity of all their employees to challenge the status quo and deliver real change. This requires health care organizations to experiment more and share their learning for the benefit of all.

7. A Call to Action

We must consistently articulate a clear call to action for everyone who works in health care. To do this we need to clearly articulate the purpose and meaning of our organizations to ensure alignment within organizations and across boundaries. In addition, clear communication will inspire contributions to the mission from the bottom up in a way that ensures every person is moving toward the same common goals.

8. Fostering an Open Culture

A commitment to transparency and openness creates a more positive environment. Openness allows learning to be shared across boundaries and shows the people we serve and our colleagues that we have integrity.

The most open organizations are the most innovative.

9. Nurturing Our People

We need to prioritize the training and development of health care staff. However, we cannot be stuck in traditional mind-sets but must develop the right mix of skills in the right places.

This would support and nurture our people to take local leadership of the changes that are needed.

10. Seeing the Bigger Picture

Teams and individuals need to be given the space and freedom to make long-term improvement plans; large changes cannot happen overnight, and we will only be able to dramatically improve the health of populations by successfully planning for the future.

11. Thought Diversity

Organizations that value dissenting opinions as much as coherence and conformity are more effective at creating change; thought diversity allows the creativity of our people to flourish and good ideas to be discovered.

The final 16 solutions (Health Services Journal 2015; Gbadamosi 2015b) were developed by staff at all levels across the NHS, from ward nurses to senior managers, and they ranged from complex ideas, such as redesigning the NHS Change Model, to simple ones, such as giving staff time to undertake change work. However, the real success of this work is not necessarily in the number or the quality of the solutions; rather, it is in the level of engagement and the strength of the voice of the crowd.

Helen Bevan, chief transformation officer at NHS Improving Quality, judged the success by three metrics (Bevan 2015):

- The first metric is the extent to which the contribution has provided a platform for many, many people to influence change and have a voice. A total of 3,595 people have joined in with the Change Challenge, making 13,895 contributions. Most of these are people who have never taken part in anything like a nationwide innovation quest before. The engagement and quality of the debate has shown how seriously people take change and how much they want to play their part in improving the NHS and the wider care system.

- The second metric is the spirit of the contributions. They were anonymous, so people could write whatever they liked. A look at the comments people make more generally on the websites of the *HSJ* and the *Nursing Times* on an anonymous basis show that the ratio of critical/challenging to positive is typically around 80:20. For the Change Challenge, this ratio was reversed; more than 80 percent of comments were affirmative. This shows how optimistic and constructive people are when they are given a chance to join in. Too often, change in the NHS gets imposed from the top down and people kick back against it.
- The third metric is the quality of the contributions. The list of "building blocks" and "barriers" for change, socially constructed by our contributors, is as good as any list of factors for change published by the *Harvard Business Review* or by major change "gurus." This supports the new era of thinking that we need to curate our own solutions (Bevan and Fairman 2014). The 16 "ideas for change" are practical solutions that could be adopted by any team or organization to make a difference. Some of them could be the first steps of challenging and transforming the culture of change in our organizations.

Summary

The philosophy and methods of the Change Challenge could be adopted by any organization or system across the country to improve the way it implements change. You could create your own local Change Challenge to design new models of care or a new urgent care strategy. If your experience is anything like ours, thousands of people will join in, will come up with ideas you hadn't even dreamed of, and will develop greater ownership of the change because they were given the opportunity to take part.

The Change Challenge was the first countrywide experiment to build a platform to capture the "wisdom of the crowd" addressing an important topic in the health care system in the United Kingdom. The era of the change platform has truly arrived.

References

Bevan, H. (2015) "Now Put the Change Challenge into Practice," http://www.hsj.co.uk/5083626.article#.VXpwQNJMvIU.

Bevan, H., and S. Fairman. (2014) "The New Era of Thinking and Practice in Change and Transformation, NHS Improving Quality," http://www.nhsiq.nhs.uk/resource-search/publications/white-paper.aspx.

Clever Together (2015) "Change Challenge Methodology," http://clevertogether.com/public/healthcare/change-challenge-methodology/.

Gbadamosi, N. (2015a) "Why Change Must Come from the Bottom Up," *Health Services Journal*, http://www.hsj.co.uk/leadership/change-challenge/why-change-must-come-from-the-bottom-up/5083572.article?blocktitle=More-from-Resource-Centre&contentID=16043#.VXmS2vlVikp.

Gbadamosi, N. (2015b) " Change Challenge: The Findings in Full," *Health Services Journal* http://www.hsj.co.uk/change-challenge-the-findings-in-full/5083699.article#.VXpvxNJMvIV.

Hamel, G. (2014) "Why Bureaucracy Must Die." *Harvard Business Review*, November 4, 2014.

Health Services Journal (2015) "Interactive Toolkit," http://www.hsj.co.uk/leadership/change-challenge/change-challenge-interactive-toolkit/5083743.article?blocktitle=More-from-Resource-Centre&contentID=16043.

Thomond, P. (2015) "Change Challenge: How It Worked," *Health Service Journal,* http://www.hsj.co.uk/leadership/change-challenge/change-challenge-how-it-worked/5083694.article?blocktitle=More-from-Resource-Centre&contentID=16043#.VXpsmtJMvIV.

CHAPTER 4

Exploring Readiness for Change and Transitions

"We must seek to create adaptive minds that respond to change with excitement and accountability."—Braden Kelley

Surveying the Change Landscape

- Change doesn't happen in isolation and often there is more change going on in an organization than any single change leader or project manager may even be aware of.
- Do you know what other change initiatives are currently underway in your organization?

Careful, be sure and include every project underway in your tally if possible, because after all every project changes something, and some of the resources that you will need for your project or change initiative are likely required to execute one or more of the other change efforts or projects.

- Have you made a list of all of the other projects and change initiatives already underway or about to start?
- Have you identified the resources in use by those projects and change efforts that you might need?
- If not, get started.

Are You Ready for Change?

Too often organizations define the change effort they want to pursue without first identifying whether there are people, resources, legislation, or other circumstances that must be in place before the change effort can begin. We will explore things you may want to consider before beginning any change implementation and the items to explore as potential prerequisites to your change program and its eventual success.

During the course of any change effort many different challenges will show themselves, and the most successful change efforts anticipate those challenges and have a plan for dealing with them. Part of that anticipation begins with identifying how ready the organization is for change and understanding what some of the top challenges are.

In a 2008 global CEO study[1] conducted by IBM on the enterprise of the future, the top challenges to successfully implementing strategic change were identified as:

1. changing mindsets and attitudes (58 percent)
2. corporate culture (49 percent)
3. underestimating complexity (35 percent)
4. shortage of resources (33 percent)
5. lack of commitment from higher management (32 percent)
6. lack of change know-how (20 percent)
7. lack of motivation of employees involved (16 percent)

You will notice that many of the items on this list are more about the human factors of change rather than the technical or process factors of change. The weight of the human dimensions of change is reflected in my PCC Change Readiness Framework (shown in figure 4.1), which is focused on the psychology of key groups concerned in the change identified, the capabilities needed to successfully execute the change, and the organization's capacity to tackle this change effort along with everything else.

You will notice there is no discussion of organizational psychology or culture in this framework. I don't highlight culture in the same way as others because in today's more social, customer-centric business we must have a wider view than the typical inward focus on company culture most authors provide. The boundaries of the organization are more porous than ever. When it comes to evaluating change readiness, we must look beyond employees and include leaders, customers, and partners too. Inevitably many of our change efforts will have some impact on one or more external groups (possibly even on the government or nonprofit entities), and we must account for this in our evaluation of change readiness.

You will notice that in the psychology box in figure 4.1 there is a common focus on the mind-sets, attitudes, beliefs, and expectations of the individuals. Culture is incorporated into the psychology realm by focusing on what the shared understandings are concerning the potential change. Finally, you will notice that the PCC Change Readiness Framework highlights that successful change efforts must move toward gaining commitment from leadership, acceptance of the change from employees, and a desire for the change from customers and partners.

In the capability box of the framework we must determine whether our change effort has any regulatory or statutory implications and whether we are ready to adapt, adopt, or influence the changes necessary in this sphere. This box also prompts us to ask ourselves the following questions:

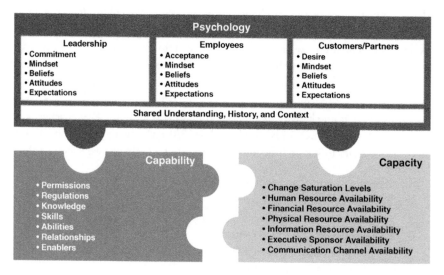

Figure 4.1   PCC Change Readiness Framework

- Do we need to get permission from anyone to do this?
- What knowledge, skills, and abilities needed for this change do we already possess?
- What knowledge, skills, and abilities needed for this change do we need to acquire?
- What relationships do we possess that will be useful in advancing the change?
- What relationships do we need to build to help advance the change?
- What are the enablers of making this change successful?

In the capacity box of the framework we have to look at where our resources are approaching or have already achieved change saturation (and are unable to productively participate in any more change efforts or adopt any more change). But we also have to look at the availability of our resources:

- human
- financial
- physical
- information
- executive sponsors
- space in our desired communication channels

It is easy to take for granted that the organization will have the capacity to undertake your change effort, but often there are capacity constraints that you will run into, especially as the pace and volume of change in an organization increases. The problem that is easiest to overlook and fail to plan for is making sure that you're going to be able to communicate your change messages in your desired messaging channels (they may already be full).

In the toolkit you will find a PCC Change Readiness Worksheet to help you explore all of these topics and more. As you work through the change process with people in your organization you'll find boxes for:

- history
- context
- shared understanding
- capability
- capacity
- leadership
- strategic alignment (commitment)
- employees
- cultural alignment (acceptance)
- partners
- customers
- brand alignment (desire)

Working through these topics in this order with your team is probably the most logical process.

When you consider all these potential stumbling blocks in advance of the change, evaluate your readiness in each area and make a plan for closing any gaps (before you even begin your change effort), you will greatly increase the chances of your effort's success. But there are certain items that are prerequisites for any change.

Prerequisites for Change

In every change effort there are certain things that must be complete before you start and certain knowledge and tools you must possess. It is helpful to look at potential prerequisites for your change effort. Ponder the following questions and capture several answers for each:

1. What must we know (knowledge)?
2. What must we have (tools)?
3. What must be completed (foundation)?

Bringing More Elements of Agile to Change

As you begin to move from the widespread chaos-driven change management model ("we do it differently every time") to using the concepts presented in this book and reinforced by use of the Change Planning Toolkit™ to spread the knowledge of how to use the collaborative, visual change planning process, you will crave a more coordinated approach to change readiness evaluation. Instead of looking at change readiness on a case-by-case basis for each individual project or change initiative, you will quickly find yourself considering the use of a more agile approach to managing change readiness. You may begin asking yourself the following questions:

1. Is it possible to have a change backlog?
2. Do we need a burndown chart to measure how quickly we are burning through our backlog?
3. Is it necessary to begin prioritizing the change backlog in order to phase in change into different parts of the organization at a pace each part can absorb?
4. Should we carve up our change initiatives into a predictable series of sprints with a regular cadence?
5. How long should our change sprints be?
6. How much of the change initiative can the organization absorb at any one time in order to maintain forward momentum?
7. Is there a need for periods of settling in (scheduled periods of equilibrium) between change sprints?
8. Is there a need for the status of various projects and change initiatives to be visible throughout the organization?

9. Is there a need for a business architect to build a business capability heatmap that highlights the amount of change impacting different business capabilities?

10. Do you have a business capability map? Do you have business architects in your organization?

If your organization is trying to become more capable of continuous change, then answering many of these questions in the affirmative and taking appropriate action will result in an accelerated change planning capability and faster change absorption.

What Change Feelings Do You Have?

Every change initiative should begin with a coordinated planning effort, and planning should always begin by surveying the landscape for change and looking both forward and backward from the current state. After having gone through the activities in the previous chapter, you will better understand the history and context of your company's change efforts. By going through the worksheets and exercises related to this chapter you will better understand what's needed and how people are thinking and feeling now; you will also gain an understanding of how they are likely to think and feel as you disrupt the status quo.

One of the worksheets you'll find in the Change Planning Toolkit™ is entitled Thinking Feeling Worksheet. Much has been written about how human beings have both a mammalian brain and a reptilian brain; put another way, we have our rational adult way of thinking about things and our emotional inner child way of feeling things (see figure 4.2).

It is often helpful to have people take a quiet moment and ask them what they first felt when they heard about the change. If they are too close to the change, you can ask them to imagine that they are one of the people most likely to be affected by the change

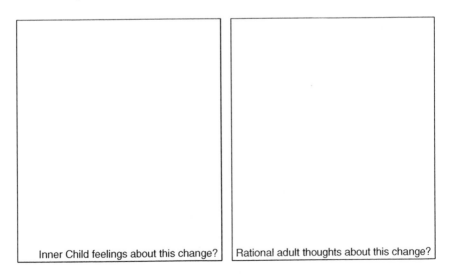

| Inner Child feelings about this change? | Rational adult thoughts about this change? |

Figure 4.2 Thinking Feeling Worksheet

and capture the feelings in the inner child box of the Thinking Feeling Worksheet. These should be feelings or empathetic feelings expressed without a filter.

Next, in your change planning workshop have people note what they thought when they heard about the change. Again, if they are too close to the change, ask them what they imagine people think about the change (both initial thoughts and more considered, informed thoughts) and note this in the box on the right in the Thinking Feeling Worksheet. Use the following questions:

- What are people's inner child feelings about this change?
- What are people's rational adult thoughts about this change?

This simple exercise helps people see that sometimes they hold two simultaneous ideas that are in conflict with each other. It also helps them identify where these thoughts and feelings may be in conflict; as change leader you can then focus some of your initial communications on accelerating the reconciliation of this conflict. The exercise above may also help you identify signals, symbols, and themes to use in these communications.

The Flow of Change

Achieving successful change is a complex undertaking, and that is why we must endeavor to make change a more human process so that it is less overwhelming for those most affected by it and for change leaders and planners as well. We can simplify change in certain ways, but we can't make it simple.

Change has been portrayed in many other change models in a far too simplistic way. For example, there it is Kurt Lewin's *Change Model*[2] with the following elements:

- unfreeze
- change
- freeze

And there is William Bridges' nearly identical *Three Phases of Transition*[3] model of:

- ending, losing, letting go
- the neutral zone
- the new beginning

A little more complexity isn't always a bad thing if it helps us go farther and achieve more, but there is a point where the complexity starts to become overwhelming. In developing a change model we can use as a guide we therefore want to strike a balance that keeps the most important detail and eliminates the least important.

The perfect balance lies in the Flow of Change Model v1.5 shown in figure 4.3. As you look at the flow of change, it is important to consider how change naturally occurs in your organization as you review your group's change readiness.

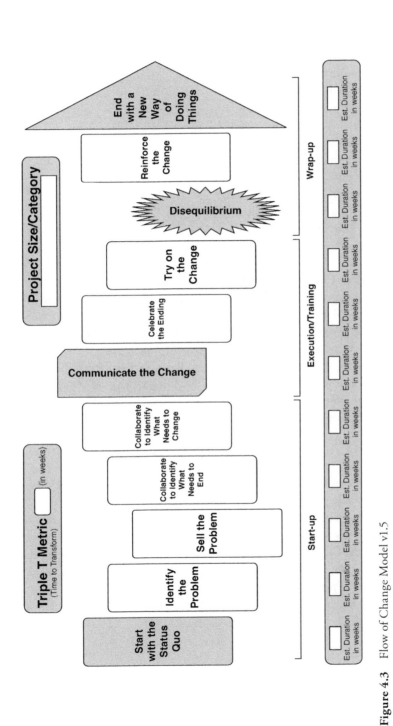

Figure 4.3 Flow of Change Model v1.5

Notice that there are not three, but eleven different distinct stages to strike the proper balance between simplicity and complexity. The eleven stages in the Flow of Change Model v1.5 illustrated in figure 4.3 are as follows:

1. Start with the status quo
2. Identify the problem
3. Sell the problem
4. Collaborate to identify what needs to end
5. Collaborate to identify what needs to change
6. Communicate the change
7. Celebrate the ending
8. Try on the change
9. Persist through disequilibrium
10. Reinforce the change
11. End with a new way of doing things

You will see that the Disequilibrium stage is shown as a starburst because this is the stage where many change efforts fail. The organization has begun ending the old way of doing things (and potentially even celebrated that ending) and has tried doing things the new way. This leads to a feeling of disequilibrium in most people as they determine whether the new way is better and decide whether they feel justified in continuing to resist the new way or whether to acclimate to doing things the new way.

Because it is important to understand the different stages of change and where your change effort currently lies, we will refer to the Flow of Change Model v1.5 at various points throughout the book.

Managing Disequilibrium and Transitions

Preparing for the disequilibrium stage and its inherent messiness is critical to protect people from additional unnecessary change.

Managing the transitions between the old way and the new way requires identifying as many transition points as possible. We must also identify the benefits of changing and those of maintaining the status quo. Then we must work together as a change planning team to find the appropriate communications content and methods to help people feel comfortable in making each transition. During this time it is helpful to look at the following elements from the PCC Change Readiness Framework:

- mind-set
- expectations
- beliefs
- attitudes
- shared understandings

Rather than overwhelming people by listing all the reasons for change at once in your communications, consider planning your communications based on a series of transitions. Frame your messages so they will help people through each transition. After all, any change is ultimately achieved through the successful completion of a number of transitions during which the individuals affected make a number of small changes in behavior that result in outcomes different from what is currently being achieved.

Measuring Organizational Agility

Coupled with the increasing interest in organizational agility is a lack of understanding about what organizational agility is and how it can be achieved. It is important therefore to define what we mean by the term.

BusinessDictionary.com has a decent definition:

> The capability of a company to rapidly change or adapt in response to changes in the market. A high degree of organizational agility can help a company to react successfully to the emergence of new competitors, the development of new industry-changing technologies, or sudden shifts in overall market conditions.[4]

People with a strong interest in organizational agility hope that this agility will help their organization cope with the increasing pace of change.

But even if you take steps to increase the agility of your organization, how will you know whether your organizational agility is improving?

Organizational agility is determined by how fast the organization is able to process and absorb change. Because organizations are struggling to understand where their greatest challenges are in coping with change and are looking for a way to measure organizational agility, I have created the Triple T Metric and incorporated it into the Flow of Change Model v1.5 shown in figure 4.3. The Triple T Metric is an acronym linked to what it measures:

Time

to

Transform

The Triple T Metric measures how long it takes an organization to make a transformation. But to measure your progress on the Triple T Metric over time, you must establish a baseline and continue to measure progress in a consistent manner. In addition, if a transformation is like a trip from point A to point B, we must define those points.

- Point A = the point in time at which the organization recognizes a change away from the steady state is needed.
- Point B = the point in time at which the organization successfully arrives at a new temporary steady state.

You'll notice that point A is not the point at which people *agree* that a change is needed and *agree* to make it. Rather, point A is the point when an organization *recognizes* a change is needed. Thus, there is a great opportunity to increase your organizational agility by increasing the speed at which your organization moves from recognizing the need for change from the status quo to agreeing to change and on to planning and executing the change and reinforcing the new way of doing things.

Figure 4.3 shows how the Flow of Change Model v1.5 breaks down the time to transform (Triple T Metric) into its component stages so that you get insight during your change planning into how long each component stage might take. In addition, you can also measure your overall progress and your stage-specific progress over time on roughly equivalent change efforts. For the Triple T Metric to work as a progress metric you'll have to categorize each change initiative or project into consistent categories based on size and/or type of change.

Consistently using the Flow of Change Model v1.5 and its Triple T Metric as part of your change planning and measurement processes will give you the ability to tell whether your organizational agility is increasing or not.

Summary

In this chapter we looked at a variety of tools from the Change Planning Toolkit™ to help you better understand your organization's current change readiness. We surveyed the change landscape to see what other projects and change initiatives might already be underway and compete with yours for resources and attention. We looked at some of the top challenges to successfully implementing strategic change and the PCC Change Readiness Framework as a way to help you evaluate some of the key focus areas as you evaluate where your organization is ready for change—in terms of psychology, capability, and capacity—and where it is not. We also looked at what some of the prerequisites for change might be to keep you see from stumbling before you even begin. Then we looked at how people can hold two conflicting ideas simultaneously and how to use the Thinking Feeling Worksheet from the toolkit. This worksheet may also help you identify useful signals, symbols, and themes to use in your communications. Next we looked at different change models, along with the eleven stages of my new Flow of Change Model v1.5 and saw how its Triple T Metric can measure potential improvements in organizational agility. Finally, we investigated the importance of the disequilibrium stage and of managing the various transitions that occur as your change efforts progress through the eleven different stages.

CHAPTER 5

Envisioning the Desired State

"You change the world every day. The real question is whether you are changing it for better or worse."—Braden Kelley

Where Do We Want to Go?

Between 1994 and 2002, Microsoft used the slogan "Where do you want to go today?"[1] and as expected some people actually rang up the company and answered the rhetorical question. The slogan was meant to convey that Microsoft software empowers people to go new places and do new things. It's no coincidence that this is exactly what change does.

But organizational change (or even a project) is not a solo journey, and so you have to develop a clear picture of where you want to go and how you plan to get people to go along with you. To do this successfully we must recognize that there is always some kind of pain associated with change, and we must overcome the inertia this inevitable discomfort or inconvenience evokes and perpetuates.

We must resist the temptation to assume that with our brilliant logic everyone will *see* the potential benefits in the change; the reality is that when faced with change, most people will instead *feel* the potential pain of the change and see nothing. So we must work to not only clarify where we want to go (our desired state), but also how we plan to facilitate the transitions people must make in order to begin doing things the new way.

Focusing on the Future

So, as you stand in the current state and look toward the desired state, focus on the future and seek to understand:

1. Who will benefit from the new way of doing things and how?
   - Who will have the power?
   - Who will have the knowledge?
   - Who will have the expertise?
   - Who will have a job as a result?
   - Are government agencies involved?
2. What are the high-level benefits of creating a new way of doing things?
   - Business benefits
   - Customer benefits
   - Employee benefits
   - Benefits to society
3. Who will lose as a result of the new way of doing things (desired state)?
   - Who will lose power?
   - Who will lose knowledge?

- Who will lose expertise?
- Who will lose a job?
- Will anyone outside the organization lose anything?

4. Have people tried to achieve this desired state before?
   - How?
   - What were the results?
   - Is anyone still around who was involved with that effort?

As we stand in the present and look forward, we will also want to remember our thoughts on the following questions:

5. Why change now?
   - The status quo was acceptable for a while. Why is it now unacceptable?
   - What are the change drivers?
6. What are the elements of context either supporting or fighting against the change?
   - Changes in the economic environment
   - Changes in the organizational psychology
   - Changes in the regulatory environment,
   - Changes in the competitive environment.
7. Who are the main proponents of this change?
   - Are they the same people feeling the bulk of the pain?
8. Where is the bulk of the change likely to take place?
9. What will happen if we don't change?
10. What will success look like?
11. How will we measure success?

Picturing the Desired State

Now is a good time to revisit what people drew in the Pictures of Today and Tomorrow worksheet we discussed earlier. Now that we've looked at the current state and your organization's change readiness, you might see what people drew in their desired state picture with new eyes, and people might even find themselves wanting to redraw what they have drawn earlier. Have some spare printouts of the Pictures of Today and Tomorrow worksheet available in case there is enough interest in redrawing the desired state.

There is nothing wrong with people changing their mind about what the desired state should look like, but be sure and ask people the reasons for their change and what they added, subtracted, enhanced, or diminished in their drawing.

If people opt to redraw their desired state, consider also having people circulate and add their comments on what they notice about the before and after pictures. These comments will likely mirror the artist's own intentions but may also surface other changes in the mind-set of the group about what the desired state should be.

Be sure to also capture potential signals, symbols, and themes in these conversations that the change planning team might be able to utilize in change communications.

Capturing the Desired State in Words

After you have asked people to revisit and possibly redraw their pictures of today and tomorrow, they should be better equipped to describe the desired state in detail. One way to capture the specifics of the desired state is to leverage the Desired State Worksheet from the toolkit, which utilizes a clear focusing theme around the following questions:

- Who?
- What?
- When?
- Where?
- Why?

In the Focusing on the Future section above you'll find several guiding questions to start the dialogue regarding each word here.

Start Stop Continue

One of the tools we've included in the Change Planning Toolkit™ is a very simple one. It's called the Start Stop Continue Worksheet (see figure 5.1), and it's focused on a comparison of the current state and the desired state based on what we should stop doing, what we should start doing, and what we should continue doing. This approach is driven by the following three questions:

1. What behaviors and beliefs will the individuals and the organization need to have?
2. What behaviors and beliefs will the individuals and the organization need to stop?
3. What behaviors and beliefs should the individuals and the organization continue to have?

While this is seemingly a fairly simple exercise, its purpose is more complex. The strength of the standard stop/start/continue framework is that it causes us to focus on both the desired stated and the current state (the status quo) at the same time. This is important is as we look to craft the desired state. It is just as important to choose what elements of the status quo will become part of the new way of doing things as it is to choose which elements of the status quo we must plan transitions for. Then we layer on top of that the behaviors and beliefs the organization will need to begin having.

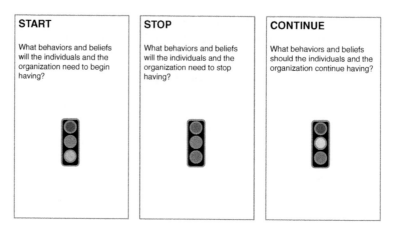

Figure 5.1 Start Stop Continue Worksheet

Forcing people to discuss what to stop, start, and continue will help surface hidden assumptions, potential barriers you may not have anticipated, and transitions you may have overlooked. The items that appear in the stop box on the Start Stop Continue Worksheet form the basis of the endings you will need to plan for. The items that appear in the continue box are the elements of comfort that you can tap into as needed, and the items that appear in the start box will likely become the focus of training initiatives.

Prototyping Change

In many cases you may find it beneficial to prototype the change before rolling it out to all of the individuals potentially affected. It is hoped that this kind of change planning process will make team members more comfortable with the idea of change. The prototype can be produced with simple physical mockups of a changed service experience or process (with physical locations or handoffs to visualize the virtual ones) or with paper prototypes of system changes or with any other method that will help make the proposed change as real as possible for the change planning team.

Getting reactions from your constituents on your proposed changes via prototyping can be an impactful way to validate assumptions and to make quick course corrections before you bring all of your resources to bear on your change plan. Intuit is famous for jumping on trains with paper prototypes of software interface modifications or with new products the company is considering introducing in order to get real-time feedback from consumers. The company does all of this prior to putting the wheels in motion for the changes necessary to code new features or user interfaces changes into their software.

Some companies, such as Kaiser Permanente and Chick-Fil-A, have built physical spaces they use for testing potential changes before they make them in their actual restaurant or hospital locations. Chick-Fil-A calls its experimental space "Hatch." The company uses this space to house a 3D virtual reality system for conducting virtual walk-throughs of experimental restaurant changes before testing them with physical prototypes. Finally, for the most promising changes the company has full test restaurant spaces and equipment (complete with observational cameras) that can be used to bring in real customers to run through simulations with actual restaurant associates to see how the changes impact the customer and employee experiences. The cameras allow Chick-Fil-A employees to monitor the customer and employee flows and performance compared to their hypotheses, and if necessary they can pause the simulations and make any real-time adjustments they want to make, before restarting the simulation.

One of the major benefits to prototyping the change you as change leader are considering making is that it helps to surface assumptions you are making in how the desired state will be achieved. Working with the prototype may also help you recognize that some of the benefits of change that you originally thought might be easy for people to understand and support actually prove difficult to understand. Alternatively, you may uncover additional reasons for resistance that you might have missed or underestimated in the beginning.

The more real you can make the prototype of the potential change as you imagine the desired state, the better the members of the change planning team will be able to understand the changes required to achieve the desired state, and the stronger your case will be to the rest of the organization regarding the merit of the change.

Once you have your change prototyped (which should also include completely populating the Change Planning Canvas^{TM}), then consider inviting both some potentially affected employees and some potentially affected customers to get their reactions to how you have defined the problem. They can also comment on your best early vision of what the desired state and the new way of doing things might look like.

Listen carefully to employee and customer feedback on your change prototype as they will likely provide information that will either confirm or overturn your assumptions, and that feedback may also help to confirm or expand the roster of potential barriers and areas of resistance you've already identified. Be sure to also test some of the other components of your completed Change Planning Canvas^{TM}, including benefits, risks, and negative impacts.

Summary

In this chapter we looked at a couple of tools from the Change Planning Toolkit^{TM} that can help you get a clearer picture of what you want the desired state to look like. We talked about the importance of understanding where you want to go and of remaining focused on the future during this phase of the change planning process. It is also important to answer the questions that will help you better shape the desired state. In this chapter we also recommended that you have your team members revisit their illustrations from the Pictures of Today and Tomorrow Worksheet and potentially redraw their picture of tomorrow. In addition, we looked at the Start Stop Continue Worksheet; this seems fairly self-explanatory and simple, but it is a powerful tool. And finally we concluded by discussing the importance of prototyping your change in whatever way you can to make sure your vision of reality will help you reach your goals and that hidden assumptions and resistance have an opportunity to surface.

Guest Expert

Seth Kahan (@sethkahan)

Seth Kahan is an executive advisor who guides CEOs on leading change and innovation to create powerfully positive impact.

www.VisionaryLeadership.com

Generating Dramatic Surges of Progress

The key to creating powerful moves forward in any initiative is to have a structure that integrates fully differentiated activity on many interdependent fronts. I first discovered this as part of the group that introduced Knowledge Management to the World Bank in the mid-1990s.

We brought together people and organizations who had many different agendas, from privatizing education to generating new centers of vitality in urban environments. The topics could not have been more varied. Yet, we found that community, a group of people who shared a common passion, was the core enabler for success. So we built communities—120 in two years around the globe. Those communities worked side-by-side with partners on many fronts: private sector, nongovernmental organizations (NGOs), international development groups, and citizen activists.

Envision a social network with many nodes and connectors. Some of those nodes were corporations. Some were individuals. Some were government agencies. Some were entrepreneurial start-ups. Each node was unique, with its own sense of purpose or mission.

We never told those involved what to do. We did not do project planning or map out milestones. Instead, we met with the participants and had conversations where we developed a common sense of what needed to be done, and we shared our conversations widely, publishing them anywhere we could and inviting as many people as possible to participate. We had open-source interaction with a common set of goals.

All of our work revolved around the common axis of poverty alleviation. Yet, as you met each party involved, it became clear that based on their unique perceptions, strengths, circumstances, and relationships each had a different view of exactly how poverty was to be alleviated.

Yet, after only two years of doing this kind of work it became clear that the impact was dramatic and powerful. In the confusing world of international development two years are like the blink of an eye. Yet, not only did the World Bank receive international recognition for its knowledge management around the globe, it became clear to our board of directors that it was an extraordinarily effective means to achieve our strategic objectives. That was my first exposure to this program.

Today I work with consortiums of leaders focused on common goals and the same principles apply. At the heart are two important principles: differentiation and integration. This is made possible with one important process: social construction.

Differentiation means that each player gets to define his or her own terms as long as that definition is in sync with the larger movement. For example, a three-person NGO gets to have its unique strategy and is not coerced into adopting the same metric as a government ministry. The integrity of each is embraced.

Integration means that there is a larger framework everyone participates in. This framework can be as loose as an annual gathering and a statement of intent or as formal as a Balanced Scorecard activity where each project is systematically updated to reflect progress or lack thereof. Either way, linkages allow information to travel to where it is needed most and can be acted on by passionate individuals.

The process, social construction, means building meaning together. This most often takes place through dialog and interaction, engaged conversation in which people have the opportunity to question, challenge, develop ideas together, disagree, and create relevant complexity. At the same time they are taking part in a common experience that becomes part of their joint history and binds them through their discussion and decisions to a way forward that makes use of everyone's contributions.

When these three pieces come together, the speed and power of results can boggle the mind. The groups that do this work together, from individuals to large organizations, achieve a collective unity that is unparalleled. As a result, actions can take place that move too fast to see what caused them; they emerge from joint understanding and simultaneous agency. The results exceed what top-down change mandates can accomplish.

Just as a flock of birds taking flight gracefully exceed any detailed attempt to orchestrate lift-off by providing individual direction to each bird, this kind of integrated, collective movement delivers extraordinary results. It appears to be coordinated by a larger intelligence. Perhaps it is.

CHAPTER 6

Picking the Right Target for Your Change Effort

"If we are to achieve results never before accomplished, we must expect to employ methods never before attempted."—Sir Francis Bacon

Put Your Change Effort on Course for Success

Every change effort must be based on knowing whose behavior is intended to be changed, and this must be clear to the change planning team and the change leaders and managers.

Sometimes we may think we know who the change is for, but if we engage in more visual and collaborative change planning efforts, we may find that the group we thought we were targeting may not be the right target or the first target or the only target in order to achieve the intended outcomes.

Often there are several potential targets for any change effort, and the group we choose to target first can accelerate or destroy the whole change effort. Targeting a group without first understanding its relative size and importance and motivations compared to other potential targets is a recipe for disaster. We must investigate the implications of targeting different potential groups with our change efforts, and we must find out how strongly each group supports or opposes the change. This means that during change planning you must segment your audience before choosing a target. We'll speak more about audience segmentation later in this chapter.

In this chapter, we will introduce tools for exploring whether your change efforts are going in the right direction and whether there might be other people you might want to target (or at least consider the impact of the change on them).

Targeting Change

The idea behind the Change Target Worksheet (see figure 6.1) is to give you one place where you can identify all the different groups of people inside and outside your organization that will be affected by the proposed change. Through conversation and collaboration based on the worksheet, you might identify some groups not previously considered (thanks to the different perspectives present in the room) and also their relative size and importance to the success of the change effort. In addition, the worksheet can help you identify groups you have thought of as one homogenous group but that really need to be split into two or more separate groups because of the heterogeneous strategies or communications you might deploy.

There are four starter questions for you to consider on this worksheet (you might come up with more):

1. Who are we making this change for?
2. Who will feel the greatest change benefit?
3. Why should this person or group be the target?
4. What motivates this group's behavior?

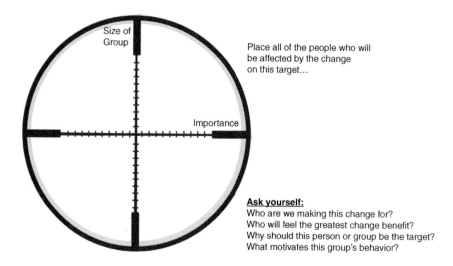

Place all of the people who will be affected by the change on this target...

Ask yourself:
Who are we making this change for?
Who will feel the greatest change benefit?
Why should this person or group be the target?
What motivates this group's behavior?

Figure 6.1 Change Target Worksheet

By writing down the groups on sticky notes and placing them on the worksheet, discussing their placement and answering the questions, you will not only identify the different groups that will be affected by the change effort, but you will also develop additional ideas about:

1. why they might resist
2. why they might support the effort
3. where they will have concerns
4. the transitions that they might struggle most with
5. what kinds of communications you might need to create for them
6. how you might best help each individual in the group transition his or her behavior from the old way of doing things to the new

Segmenting the Change Audience

One way to begin documenting the natural audience segments for your communications to advance your change effort from idea to successful completion is to use the Change Audience Segmentation Worksheet from the Change Planning Toolkit™.

There are two worksheets in the toolkit that provide you with space to capture the segment characteristics and potential messaging components for up to eight different audience segments. One strategy for filling out the Change Audience Segmentation Worksheets (or to otherwise capture and organize your segmentation data) is to duplicate the sticky notes you created and affixed to the Change Target Worksheet and begin grouping the sticky notes together into logical segments. Then the group can begin brainstorming different key themes, symbols, signals, and messages for these different segments.

Participants in your session may also find that the number of segments grows or shrinks as they work their way through the conversations required to complete the worksheet and identify segments that they have perhaps defined too broadly or two narrowly. One segment might need to be split into two or more because subgroups need significantly different messages. Or perhaps the change planning team has defined a segment too narrowly and finds the messages a particular segment will need are very similar to those for another segment, and the team may then decide creating a separate version of the communications is not worth the effort. The goal of segmenting your change audience is to find the segments that are so different as to require a strategy and communications different from those for the others in order to drive the desired change outcomes within that segment. Ultimately, this effort works in support of broader success across all of the segments and thus the desired outcomes in total.

Summary

In this chapter we looked at a couple of tools from the Change Planning Toolkit™ you can use to help you ensure that you are targeting the right groups with your change effort (and also to make sure you haven't missed any that might be impacted). This way you can segment the change audience for the eventual creation of a communications plan complete with key messages, symbols, signals, and themes. We have also investigated the implications of targeting the selected groups for your change efforts and whether or not they want this change.

When you take the time to do these things rather than assuming the same messages, symbols, signals, and themes will work for everyone, the chances increase that your change effort will be successful. And success is also more likely when you don't assume that you have already identified the intended change target(s) correctly and haven't left any important constituencies out.

Identifying the players and what they care about now will set you up to do better work on the people side of change in the upcoming chapters and will help you investigate the change benefits and negative outcomes that might accrue to the change targets you have identified in this chapter.

CHAPTER 7

The Benefits of Change

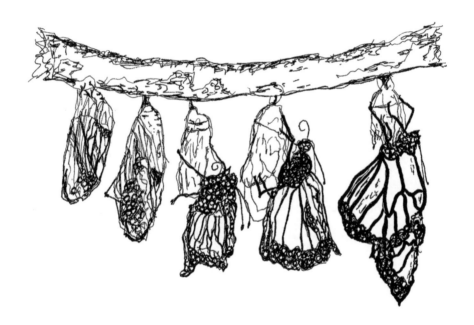

"If you do not create change, change will create you."—Unknown

Looking at the Positive Side of Change

Every change creates both positive and negative outcomes. The positive outcomes are the benefits of undertaking the change effort. Some of these benefits will be obvious, but there may be other benefits that are important to certain segments of your change audience but may be just beneath the surface and not obvious; or people may refuse to recognize some benefits. The goal of this section is to help you think through the different potential benefits of your change effort for all your constituencies. In this chapter we will therefore focus on the positive elements of change for several constituencies, including:

1. benefits to partners and to the organization
2. gains employees might incur
3. any positive outcomes for customers the change effort might generate

We will look at a selection of tools from the toolkit and a couple of case studies to help you capture, group, and prioritize the potential benefits.

The Benefits Worksheet

In the toolkit you will find a Benefits Worksheet (see figure 7.1) that will help you organize the group's thoughts as you brainstorm potential benefits of the proposed change and how they affect customers, employees, partners (including suppliers), and the business itself.

Here are some customer benefits to get your thinking started:

- Lower price?
- Better customer service?
- Easier to do business?
- More value?

Here are a few employee benefits to get your thinking started:

- Happier?
- Less frustration?
- Higher retention?

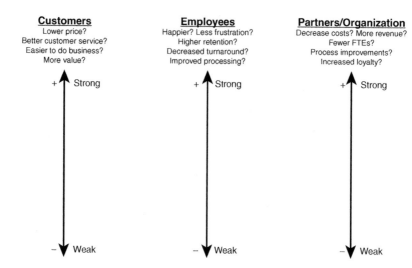

Figure 7.1   Benefits Worksheet

- Decreased turnaround?
- Improved processing?

And finally, here are some potential benefits for the organization or its partners to get your thinking started:

- Decrease costs?
- Increase revenue?
- Fewer full-time employees (FTEs)?
- Process improvements?
- Increased loyalty?

As you will see in figure 7.1, as people come up with ideas for potential benefits they will want to write them down on sticky notes and then place them up on the worksheet under the appropriate heading (customers, employees, or partners/organization).

You will also see on the Benefits Worksheet that you'll want to encourage people to estimate the strength of the impact (from "weak" to "strong"). Once the pace of sticky note placement slows to a trickle, then you can ask for any last submissions and then read out all of the sticky notes placed in a single category and group those that are identical or nearly identical on top of each other. Then ask the group whether the impact should be higher or lower than where it is (or whether it is perfect where it is). The goal here is not to remove duplicates, but to cluster similar benefits and to rank all the benefits based on their relative strength or weakness.

Ten Benefits of Change That Are Easy to Miss

When we are thinking about making organizational change or a project that will change something, it is easy to miss some of the benefits of a potential change that might be more personal:

1. personal growth
2. an increasingly flexible organization over time
3. creation of new opportunities
4. a chance for a new beginning
5. escape from boredom and monotony
6. creation of new ways of thinking
7. opportunity for employees to show off hidden capabilities
8. creating a learning organization over time
9. chance to get ahead of the crowd
10. increased energy and creativity
11. <insert your favorite unexpected or personal benefit of change here>

Start Over or Running Start?

Every change effort is a chance to ask one of the most powerful questions in business: Given how things are going now, do we change what we are doing now, or do we begin doing things in a completely new way as if we were beginning again?

This leads naturally to a second question: Do we have permission to completely destroy the status quo and design a completely different way of doing things (effectively starting over or acting like a start-up choosing how to do something for the first time), or do we need to evolve the way we currently do things gradually to a new way of doing things?

Most of the time designing a new way of doing things with a clean slate won't even be an option, but we should always ask that question so we know what options we have for creating a new way of doing things (the desired state) and how much of the status quo will have to be part of the new way of doing things.

Unexpected Benefits of Change

Every change we advocate for will almost always bring unexpected benefits (and potentially unexpected negative outcomes too) as we move to implement the change. Here are a couple of examples of change initiatives big and small that have resulted in unexpected benefits.

First example (Sarbanes Oxley)[1]: If we look back to the Sarbanes-Oxley Act (SOX) of 2002, most of the chatter in the media was about how the act was going to burden businesses with additional costs that could run into the millions of dollars and take their executives' attention away from more important matters. But as

SOX became law, more and more executives were shocked by the gaps and weaknesses exposed by assessments and compliance reviews, including a feeble compliance culture, unnecessary complexity, inadequate enforcement of existing policies, and insufficient and unclear communications. Executives who recognized SOX's advantages from the beginning have figured out how to leverage the new law to force the implementation of previously stalled plans for improvement.

A business environment of strengthened control may have been one of the main expected benefits of SOX, but the act has also led to improved documentation, increased involvement of audit committees, converged controls, standardized processes, reduced complexity, stronger intracompany relationships, and fewer manual processes. Many of these benefits brought to organizations by SOX were unexpected, but welcome nonetheless.

Second example (school fundraisers): Here in the United States, there is an almost endless march of children to our doors throughout the year as they engage in some kind of school or social group (Girl Scouts, Boy Scouts, etc.) fundraiser. As a parent of a child who has come home trying to get family members and friends to buy the inevitable lottery ticket or sugary trinket, I've found myself tempted to just write a check to get my daughter out of having to participate. But while this may seem an easier way out than following your kids around the neighborhood as they ring doorbells and try to get people to buy stuff for the fundraiser of the week, there are actually unexpected benefits of this change activity that the school or social group is engaging in. among the benefits are the following:

- building confidence in children as they successfully use their communication skills;
- raising children's self-esteem as they set goals and exceed them,
- teaching kids that it's okay to ask for help;
- instilling a work ethic and enhancing children's entrepreneurial skills;
- increased children's creative problem solving skills as they are involved in every phase from identifying problems to solving them.

Linking Benefits to Motivations

Going through these exercises should unearth additional benefits that may help to energize and motivate the change planning team, and it is hoped that the conversations will also:

1. uncover additional talking points for change leaders to use in rallying others
2. help uncover clear links between benefits and motivations that can be leveraged
3. add to the list of potential messages to leverage in your targeted and segmented change communications

The better you understand the benefits, individual motivations, and potential risks and negative outcomes of your change effort, the more likely you will be to get people to choose change and help you achieve the desired change outcomes.

Summary

In this chapter we focused on why we are engaging in this change effort (or project) and the expected benefits for employees, customers, partners, and the organization. We looked at the Benefits Worksheet from the toolkit and how to use it to identify the various kinds of benefits and rank them based on their relative impact and importance.

We investigated possible unexpected benefits of change (including a couple of examples) and we looked at ten benefits of change that are easy to miss. We looked at whether we have permission to turn our change situation into a blank slate for a new start and the different ways we might achieve the desired outcomes based on this important factor. And finally, we looked at the importance of linking benefits to motivations. In the next chapter we will discuss the importance of linking the negative outcomes and risks to motivations as well.

CHAPTER 8

The People Side of Change

"Every man is an impossibility until he is born."—Ralph Waldo Emerson

The keys to success in any change program typically lie in the human elements, not in any technology components. This chapter will focus not just on the people involved in your change effort and on the people you are targeting for change, but also on the people beyond your primary change target. This includes those who can help and those who will resist your change, but we must also focus on identifying the disaffected and those people affected by the change who might not immediately come to mind. We must also look at your change team again now that we've started planning because you must make sure to have all the roles represented on the team that are needed to achieve your maximum success potential.

Who Can Help?

It is important early on as you're planning your change effort (or project) to identify the people who can help you achieve your goals for the change initiative. This is the first box in the People Worksheet from the toolkit. There are several ways that people can help you with your change effort, including the following:

1. providing history and/or context;
2. helping you gain traction by providing an endorsement or their support;
3. providing resources to advance the effort (physical, human, systems, information, knowledge, access to communication channels, etc.);
4. helping to evangelize for the change effort;
5. lending influence to help remove obstacles;
6. providing feedback on your Change Planning Canvas™ before you share it more broadly;
7. joining your team.

Change is (and should be) a collaborative experience. The goal should be to make people feel that the organization is planning and executing change as a joint effort, rather than that change is something being done to them.

Nearly everyone aside from the Real Time Strategic Change (RTSC) proponents, people who think the entire organization should be involved in planning and executing the change, believes that change should be planned by a core group of individuals from several levels and functions in the organization before it is rolled out to the rest of the organization.

But there is a danger in approaching change in this manner, namely, the aforementioned chance that people might feel that change is being done to them instead of by them. One of the keys to avoiding this pitfall is identifying early on who can help your change effort succeed; then you must work to get these people involved in the planning process, the execution phase, or both.

Looking at this area of potential risk through the lens of The Eleven Change Roles™ will give you a better chance of identifying and including people who can help you because your field of view on the potential ways that people could help will be wider.

Revisiting The Eleven Change Roles™

In chapter 2, "Planning Change," we introduced The Eleven Change Roles™ as part of a section on identifying the people who should be part of your change planning team. Identifying the roles to be filled up-front so that you can invite the right people to participate is important. But it is also important to revisit the roles now that you're midway through change planning efforts to make sure that you have all of the eleven roles filled both during the change planning process and as you move forward into the execution phase. Do you have the people in your sessions with the knowledge, information, and most well-considered viewpoints on the topics you're focusing on?

By now you should have found and filled The Eleven Change Roles™ identified as important to forming a balanced and successful change leadership team. Here is a reminder of the different roles:

1. Authority Figures/Sponsors

Somebody has to be in charge. This includes one main sponsor and a coalition of authority figures who can help push things forward when a push is required.

2. Designers

Designers are your big picture thinkers, people who can see how the pieces fit together, who are skilled meeting facilitators, who know the methodology well, and who can help keep people on track as you build the plans for your change effort.

3. Influencers

Influencers are well-respected and forceful people in the organization. They may lack the formal position power of a sponsor or authority figure, but they can help rally people to the cause with their words and actions.

4. Integrators

Integrators are good at bridging silos, building relationships that cut across geographies and hierarchies, and finding ways for different teams and departments to work together to achieve a common goal.

5. Connectors

Connectors are slightly different from Integrators, and the difference is that Connectors know where the overt and hidden resources lie in the organization and have the personal connections and influence necessary to open a dialogue that can result in a needed connection.

6. Resource Controllers/Investors

These people have things you need—human resources, information resources, and physical resources. You must get them to invest those resources to successfully achieve your desired change.

7. Troubleshooters

There are always going to be problems that emerge along the way; some are expected, and some are not. Troubleshooters are really good at identifying problems early on, and they enjoy the challenge of finding ways around, over, under or through these potential barriers. It is even better when the team can identify ways to overcome problems before communications to the rest of the organization begin. Troubleshooters can help with this and often have the domain knowledge or the deep insight into the change target's mind-set necessary to also move minds and resources to support the change program.

8. Evangelists/Storytellers

Every change effort has a story to tell about how the desired future state is better than the current state and is worth the disruption of making the change. There is a vision, themes that will weave together in your story, and symbols that will reinforce and show your commitment to realizing the goals you set for the change effort. Without this evangelism and storytelling it will be really hard for people to understand what you are trying to do or to support it. So you need to have evangelists and storytellers at the ready.

9. Endorsers/Supporters

Getting people to agree to talk up the change effort even if they are not taking an active role in pushing it toward completion is very powerful. Don't be afraid to reach out and ask for this seemingly insignificant assistance, but arm these individuals with the themes, symbols, and stories that will reinforce the vision and sustain momentum.

10. The Impacted (key groups of impacted individuals)

Who is going to be affected by this change? Don't be afraid to invite these people early on to voice their concerns so that you can understand their objections, identify solutions or mitigations, and potentially recruit them as effective evangelists.

Figure 8.1 The Eleven Change Roles

11. The External (perspectives from people not affected)

It's easy to miss risks, assumptions, barriers, and points of potential resistance when you are too close to the effort. Inviting in some people from outside your organization to be part of your planning process and to get their feedback on what you are trying to do might be surprisingly enlightening as they contribute their perspective.

By recruiting people into all eleven roles listed above (and visualized below in figure 8.1), you should be gathering a rich set of inputs, having lively discussions, and generating a strong set of outputs from your change planning process. Having your team verbalize meaningful, well-intentioned, and well-informed contributions regarding the key components of the Change Planning Canvas™ should be providing powerful content as you work through the series of worksheets in the toolkit and ultimately develop your execution plans.

Who Will Resist?

People may resist your change effort for a number of different reasons, but you need to identify up-front not only *why* people may resist but also *who* will likely resist. Toolkit users will want to capture the group's thoughts on who will resist in the middle box of the People Worksheet from the toolkit.

Some of the typical reasons why people will resist include:

- inability to see the need for change or its relevance;
- loss of certainty (includes fear of job loss);

- loss of purpose, direction, or status;
- loss of mastery (includes loss of expertise/recognition);
- loss of control or ownership;
- loss of connection or attachment;
- lack of trust or clarity;
- fear of failure (feel unprepared);
- see proposed change as irrelevant or a bad idea;
- feel overwhelmed by thought of change.

You'll want to identify the individuals or groups who have one of the above reasons for resisting change, and you will want to plan from the start to overcome that resistance in the same way that any good salesperson plans for objections, learns to hear them, and practices how to overcome them (for example, by developing and sharing strategies with coworkers).

In the toolkit I've provided space in the Overcoming Resistance Worksheet for your team to brainstorm both the groups and individuals likely to feel any of these reasons for resistance, together with space to capture some ideas for overcoming these objections (aka resistance) and what the root cause of the objections might be.

Next, when it comes to your change effort, you will find that people are likely distributed in a fairly typical bell curve distribution across five different categories highlighted in figure 8.2:

1. Passionate Resistors
2. Passive Resistors
3. The Disaffected
4. Tepid Supporters
5. Strong Supporters

Other authors have made similar conjectures, with some directly lifting the methodology from Geoffrey Moore's book *Crossing the Chasm*[1] and using

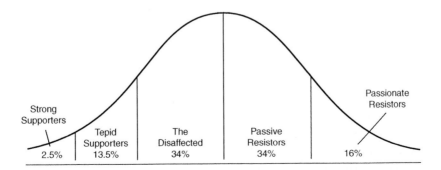

Figure 8.2 The Five Change Reactions

the terminology of early adopters, early majority, late majority, laggards, etc. The problem with approaching the acceptance of change in this way is that it would imply that you can focus only on one group at a time and that getting everyone to adopt the change will take a great deal of time as you work to convert one group after the other.

But if you look at change in the way I outline above, you can start to identify which of your segments identified in earlier worksheets are likely to cluster together into the five categories highlighted in figure 8.2 above. And then, because you have a different communications strategy for each segment, you can execute a coordinated communications plan that will allow you to begin converting several categories at once by speaking to their unique conversion needs.

Now is a good time for toolkit users to go to the Five Change Reactions Worksheet and start categorizing the groups and individuals who fall into one of the five change reaction categories. Don't worry if you cannot place every group into one of the categories because at this point you may not be sure how different groups or individuals not in the room might react to the change. That's okay. The purpose of this exercise is to highlight the different reactions and to help your teams understand why people might have one reaction or another. This will start team members thinking about how through the use of sound communications and execution strategies, some positive movement to the left from one reaction to another may be initiated.

You will find that there are two major areas of opportunity arising from the potential distribution of reactions in many change efforts:

1. converting the Disaffected into Tepid Supporters, and
2. converting Passive Resistors into the Disaffected or Tepid Supporters.

Shifting all of these people by one category would shift the percentages from 84 percent not supporting your initiative to 84 percent not opposing your initiative. Because of the importance and size of these two groups, the Disaffected and the Passive Resistors, you will want to identify people likely to fall into those categories and hone your strategies for shifting as much of the distribution to the left as possible.

Identifying the Passive Resistors and the Disaffected

One way of identifying the Disaffected and the Passive Resistors is to form a problem statement and survey different parts of the organization to see where support for the problem statement is low (i.e., areas where people are less likely to agree that this is a problem that needs to be solved) and where there is tangible disagreement that a problem exists. The surveys can be anonymous. Ideally, you will segment your audience for your change communications and survey each segment separately so that you can use any survey results to help craft the messages you send to each segment during your different change communications phases (refer to the segmentation of your change audience that you created back in chapter 6).

Identifying the groups and individuals least likely to be affected by the changes will also help you to identify the Disaffected and the Passive Resistors, as there will be a strong correlation between a group feeling no impact from the change and either being a supporter or part of the Disaffected. Conversely, the groups most likely to feel an impact from the change are most likely to fall into the supporter or resistor categories (depending on whether they view the change as having a positive or a disruptive impact on them).

Who Else Will Be Affected?

Last, consider who else will be affected. Have people take another look at the Change Target Worksheet from the toolkit (discussed in chapter 6) and the segmentation of your change audience you created previously.

By looking at your list of potential change targets you chose not to focus on and the audience segments you plan to communicate with and moving them all onto your list of who else will be affected, you may end up identifying individuals or groups that you've missed. In doing so, you might find additional individuals or groups that you may want to move to the "Who can help?" or "Who will resist?" sections of the People Worksheet.

Focusing on Achieving the Results You Seek

The results pyramid framework[2] from Tom Smith and Roger Connors' book *Change the Culture: Change the Game* highlights the importance of building a culture of accountability and introduces the idea that leaders too often focus on trying to change people's actions when seeking new results. What we can learn from Smith and Connors is that for transformational change to be lasting and sustainable, leaders must work to change the beliefs and experiences people have. They must ensure that people have new experiences that lead to new beliefs that in turn lead to new actions that ultimately support the desired results.

As you explore the behavior change you'd like to see, capture the experiences people are having with the current way of doing things, the beliefs they have as a result, the actions they are taking, and the results they get. Keep it simple by doing the following:

1. First focus on identifying the new results the group wants to achieve after making the change.
2. Second, ask employees and partners what new experiences they think people will need to have in order to leave the old way of doing things behind and to support the new results you want to achieve *and* to believe the organization is committed to the new results.

3. Third, ask what new beliefs they think people will need to have in order to commit to leaving behind the old way of doing things and to taking new actions.

4. Finally, ask what new actions they think people will need to take in order to achieve the results you are hoping for in the desired state.

In most cases you will find that your current set of experiences, beliefs, actions, and results represents a sort of equilibrium. And one of the keys to achieving successful change is to move from your current state of equilibrium or alignment to a new set of experiences, beliefs, and actions so that you can create a new state of equilibrium based on your new results. As you begin to craft a strategy for shifting people from the current state to the desired state, keep in mind Smith and Connors' case for change best practices:[3]

1. Make it real.
2. Make it applicable to your audience.
3. Make it simple and repeatable.
4. Make it convincing.
5. Make it a dialogue.

Summary

In this chapter we focused on identifying who can help, and we revisited the Eleven Change Roles™ and the contribution of each to a successful (and balanced) change team.

We also looked at who will resist, and I introduced the Five Change Reactions. I explained that identifying the Passive Resistors and the Disaffected and improving the outlook of these groups can tip the change effort from doomed to failure toward a success.

Finally, we looked at how a couple of concepts from Smith and Connors can be used to move equilibrium based on the current state in an orderly way to a new state of equilibrium based on a new set of results and supported by a new set of experiences, beliefs, and actions. These will reestablish alignment and help you achieve the goals and metrics you set out in the previous chapter.

CHAPTER 9

Barriers and Obstacles to Change

"Change is never painful; only resistance to change is painful."—Buddha

E very change effort will encounter obstacles and potential barriers that, if left unaddressed, could keep the change effort from being successful. In this chapter we will look at some of the common barriers and obstacles of change efforts and an approach that can be used to overcome them.

Different Categories of Barriers and Obstacles

There are many different barriers and obstacles that any change effort might encounter, but most barriers and obstacles fall into one of four categories highlighted on the Barriers Worksheet accessible to toolkit users. These include the following barriers and obstacles:

1. psychological/political
2. logistical
3. financial
4. external

Psychological and Political Barriers and Obstacles

Psychological and political barriers and obstacles are the ones people most often think of when they think of opposition to change. But we aren't just talking about opposition to change here; we are talking about identifying, understanding, and defeating specific barriers and obstacles that either already exist or are put into place as a defense mechanism to inhibit the forward momentum of your change effort (or project) toward its successful completion. Psychological and political barriers and obstacles occur quite frequently and include the following:

- trust level
- cultural readiness
- potential misunderstandings
- organizational politics

Logistical Barriers and Obstacles

Logistical barriers and obstacles are typically composed of items having a time-related or process-related component. These types of barriers and obstacles are often some of the easier ones to overcome because they are more logical or procedural and typically just need to be considered and planned for. Logistical barriers and obstacles include the following:

- time of year
- speed of change
- prerequisites
- resource availability

Financial Barriers and Obstacles

Financial barriers and obstacles usually involve money and often are among the most difficult barriers and obstacles to overcome because it is easy for people to hide behind the numbers. But that is not to say that there isn't room for creativity in your approach and strategies for overcoming even these barriers and obstacles. Financial barriers and obstacles usually include the following:

- budget
- competing priorities

External Barriers and Obstacles

External barriers and obstacles come from outside the organization, and as with barriers or obstacles beyond the purview of the organization(s) led by you or the members of your team, there is typically a great need for lobbying as part of your strategy for overcoming them. Typical external barriers and obstacles include the following:

- labor union work rules
- laws and regulations

Strategies for Overcoming Barriers and Obstacles

By most accounts there are four different ways to address barriers or obstacles that stand in the way of the forward progress you seek in pursuit of your desired state and its expected outcomes. Here is a list of four different ways to address an obstacle or barrier and what each approach looks like in the context of a change effort (or project):

1. *Go OVER it*
   - Find the higher ground either by identifying a person (or group of people) who can influence the individual or group acting as a blocker. Or, in the case of other kinds of barriers, ask if there is a higher level budget, strategy, law, belief, etc. that you can appeal to that will lead to a reduction

(or elimination) of power from the obstacle or barrier blocking your change effort.

2. *Go UNDER it*
   - Identify ways that you can proactively work to remove support from the barrier or obstacle or to build a strong enough opposition to it from the bottom up until the barrier or obstacle collapses before you.
3. *Go AROUND it*
   - Challenge the group to identify another path to the goal that doesn't require you to go through the obstacle or barrier you find in your way. For example, not asking for permission, but asking for forgiveness later is one approach that falls into this category.
4. *Go THROUGH it*
   - This means showing people a better way, bribing people to tear the obstacle down, or intimidating people into abandoning their posts defending the obstacle or barrier. This overpowering strategy is the riskiest of all.

You can also ask yourself whether there are similarities between this barrier or obstacle and one you have overcome before.

Process for Overcoming Barriers or Obstacles

1. *Identify*
   - The first step in the process for overcoming barriers or obstacles is identifying the type of barrier or obstacle you're facing (psychological/political, logistical, financial, or external).
   - What is the source of the barrier or obstacle?
2. *Understand*
   - The second step is to understand how the barrier or obstacle came to be where it is.
   - Who benefits from it being there?
3. *Plan (or Strategize)*
   - The third step is to look at what you've learned during the identify and understand phases of the process and then use that knowledge to pick a strategy from the "Strategies for Overcoming Barriers and Obstacles" that will help you Go OVER it, Go UNDER it, Go AROUND it, or Go THROUGH it.
4. *Probe*
   - The fourth step is to begin gently probing the barrier to find out whether your assumptions about its reason for being, its expected level of resistance, and the chances of success of your chosen strategy are relatively correct.
   - The outcomes of your probing will either lead you to feel confident in proceeding or will make you feel that your strategy needs to be fundamentally reconsidered.

5. *Attack*
   - The fifth step in the Process for Overcoming Barriers or Obstacles is to take everything that you have learned during the probe step to modify your strategy as needed and then proceed to execute it to go over, under, around, or through the obstacle or barrier in order to advance your change effort or initiative (or project) toward successful completion.
6. *Observe*
   - The sixth step occurs while you are attacking the barrier or obstacle blocking your change effort and involves observing how those defending the barrier or obstacle respond to your attack. No matter how well you orchestrate the probing activities in the fourth step, and no matter how comprehensive they are, an actual attempt to overcome a change obstacle or barrier will always elicit a response, usually an unexpected one.
7. *Respond*
   - The seventh and final step is to take those unexpected responses to your strategy for overcoming the barrier or obstacle and develop a response of your own, one that can lead you to eventual and total success in overcoming the barrier or obstacle and achievement of your change goals.

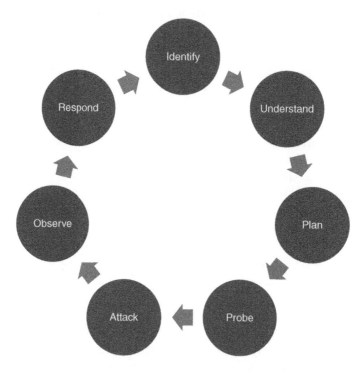

Figure 9.1 Process for Overcoming Barriers and Obstacles

After going through the seven steps of the Process for Overcoming Barriers or Obstacles (see figure 9.1) you should then have succeeded in either getting past the obstacle, or you'll realize that your strategy (or its effectiveness in successfully conquering the barrier or obstacle in question) is sufficiently flawed that you need to move through the process from the beginning again.

Summary

In this chapter we looked at how every change effort will encounter barriers and obstacles with the potential to keep the change effort from being successful. We looked at some of the common barriers and obstacles and the different categories that they typically fall into.

1. Psychological/Political
2. Logistical
3. Financial
4. External

We also looked at some strategies for overcoming barriers and obstacles.

1. Go OVER it
2. Go UNDER it
3. Go AROUND it
4. Go THROUGH it

And finally we looked at a seven-stage process you can follow to increase your chances of achieving success with your change initiative (or project).

1. Identify
2. Understand
3. Plan (or Strategize)
4. Probe
5. Attack
6. Observe
7. Respond

Guest Expert

Matthew E. May (@matthewemay)

Strategy facilitator, innovation coach, and lean trainer. Author of four books (including *The Laws of Subtraction* and *The Elegant Solution*), working on a fifth.

www.MatthewEMay.com

Reverse Engineer Your Strategy by Asking "What Must Be True?"

Your change strategy seems airtight on paper. But as the saying goes, no strategy survives first contact with the enemy. Or as Mike Tyson once quipped, "Everyone has a plan until they are punched in the face.[1]" Generally, that's because multiple assumptions have been folded into your strategy—unconscious leaps of faith you've made in your natural enthusiasm and optimistic outlook.

If not attended to, teased out, made transparent, and tested in the real world, these leaps may indeed become the very blind spots that will render your strategy a fun but ultimately academic thought experiment.

Here's the thing: your strategy is just a collection of guesses until it is tested. There is real power in making bold assumptions because you can turn them into clear hypotheses and then scientifically test them in a rapid, iterative way.

Done right, your eventual strategy will indeed survive first contact with reality. The key lies in the approach. In my experience, simply making a list of your assumptions doesn't work, for the simple reason that our assumptions are part of our mental models and biases—they're so ingrained in our thinking and thus so hard to identify that it takes a tool to make the process more objective.

We naturally tend to list "known" things for sake of ease and to avoid the risk of looking uncertain. But an assumption by definition is something unknown. And that's scary. We fear the unknown, and we are reticent to bring it up. The best technique I've found to bring assumptions out into the open is a single but powerful question: *What must be true?*

Most organizations approach strategic change by first trying to understand what is true about the world—conducting extensive analysis about their industry, their customers, their competitors, and their own capabilities. Such an analysis is time-consuming and expensive.

I learned that it is far more effective and powerful to reverse the typical order. You don't turn to analysis and testing until *after* you've articulated your strategy, and you analyze and test only the elements that are critical to moving forward.

Asking and testing what would have to be true for your strategy to be successful is best thought of as reverse engineering, because you are working from the future back to the present to identify the conditions for success. Then you can focus on the conditions that you are most worried are not true. Your most worrisome conditions, those you feel are least likely to be true, are the barriers to your eventual success.

The first step of reverse engineering is to identify the conditions that would have to be true for your strategy to be a good one. This step requires you to answer the following six key questions:

1. What must be true about the structure, size, and attractiveness of our target segments?
2. What must be true about what our end users value?
3. What must be true about what our channels value?
4. What must be true about our capabilities compared to those of our competitors?
5. What must be true about our costs compared to our competitors' costs?
6. What must be true about how our competitors will react to our strategy?

Depending on the nature and focus of your strategic change, not all of these may be directly applicable. But don't dismiss the question automatically, simply because a word or term doesn't have an obvious application to your situation. Take into consideration the thrust of the question and substitute a better word. (For example, for a strategy relating to internal change, instead of "segment" try "group" or "business unit.")

You should be able to identify a few conditions for each question. After you've captured all the answers, ask: "Of all the things that would have to be true for us to be confident in this strategic possibility, which conditions do we *most worry aren't true?*"

You'll then have a short list of two to four barriers that you can test, in order of their concern to you.

CHAPTER 10

Not Everything about Change Is Wonderful

"While there is risk to change, just like with innovation, there is often potentially more risk associated with doing nothing."—Braden Kelley

We might like to think that every outcome of a change effort is positive, but the truth is that with every change there are inevitably negative outcomes and risks that must be measured, mitigated, and managed. We will look at some of the unexpected consequences of change and the risks you may face.

It is important to state upfront that negative outcomes and risks are not the same thing. Negative outcomes are circumstances and behaviors that we are sure will impact at least some people in a negative way. Some people might have to work harder in the short term, and some people might be asked to no longer work at all. Risks, on the other hand, are circumstances and behaviors that are not certain, events that might occur or might not. While negative outcomes will happen with certainty and risks might only have a small chance of happening, both risks and negative outcomes should be identified, documented, and understood. And both are worthy of a mitigation plan to minimize the chances of a risk being realized and to minimize the impact from any risks or from expected negative outcomes.

Negative Outcomes

It is easy to imagine all of the positive outcomes from our change effort or upgrade project, but just as easy to miss the potential negative outcomes. Why is it that the Project Management Institute (PMI) implores its certified project management army to identify risks and build a mitigation plan but fails to account for the inevitable negative outcomes that every project or change initiative will generate?

The answer is easy. The litany of popular sayings that we share on Twitter or Facebook or put on posters in our hallways all emphasize that change is good and that change in the name of progress should be supported without question. So how could there be a downside to any project or change effort? Well, actually it's inevitable. So you should always ask yourself the following three questions highlighted in the Negative Impacts Worksheet (which can be used for both known negative outcomes and those negative impacts that might arise if a risk is realized):

1. Who is affected?
2. How are they affected?
3. What mitigation strategies could be employed?

Negative outcomes that you should consider include:

- an increase in technological and process/procedure complexity,
- a significant process or procedure change,

- physical relocations,
- a significant structural adjustment,
- compensation or benefit impacts,
- human resource adjustments,
- significant changes in job roles,
- a shift in the expected speed of implementation.

Of course, there are many different potential negative outcomes that may occur as the result of your change initiative (or project), but this list should help you and your group voice many other potential negative outcomes that you should consider whether or not they are likely to occur as a result of this effort. And you should think of how you might mitigate the impact of these negative outcomes.

Risks

No project or change initiative is free of risk, especially when you consider the fact that most changes will ultimately require a change in the behavior of one or more individuals. And as people begin behaving differently, they sometimes begin behaving in unanticipated ways.

If you draw a blank when thinking about the risks your project may face, start by referring to the work you did in chapter 9, "Barriers and Obstacles to Change," because there is obviously a risk that you may not be able to overcome one or more of the barriers or obstacles you have identified. Overcoming those barriers and obstacles is the basis of your mitigation strategies. And as you begin talking about the risks these barriers and obstacles represent, getting them identified and communicated on a tool like the Risks Worksheet (see figure 10.1) will start a conversation about their relative rankings for probability and impact. At the same time, such a conversation should uncover other potential risks that you will need to mitigate.

The Risks Worksheet is designed to capture the following three main things:

1. probability of the risk occurring
2. the potential impact of the risk if it should occur
3. strategies for reducing the chances of the risk occurring
   a. The Negative Impacts Worksheet is for capturing ideas on how to mitigate the negative impacts you expect to occur.

As the group's dialogue about risk continues, you will capture all the potential risks the group sees in the Risks Worksheet, and then you can focus on your mitigation strategies for each risk, especially those risks the group scores as highly probable and having a great impact.

Change Causes Ripples

One of the reasons so many change efforts fail is that people tend to underestimate the scale and breadth of the change that cascades across an organization (and

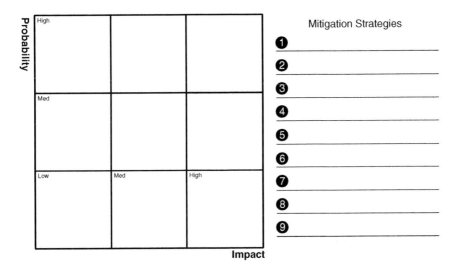

Figure 10.1   Risks Worksheet

potentially outside too) as a result of the change effort. Think for a second about the impact of the decision by Apple to create the iPhone.

This decision was probably made shortly after the failed September 2005 launch of the Motorola ROKR (Apple's first experience with the mobile phone industry). Steve Jobs didn't like to fail and after working with Motorola inevitably would have come away feeling that to be successful Apple would need to own the entire experience. This single decision impacted the company's talent requirements in a big way. Apple now had a need for people who knew about the carrier ecosystem, handset manufacturing, mobile phone hardware design, mobile phone software design, and other such specific knowledge the company did not have available in-house at the time. On the other hand, this only represents the change ripple effecting Human Resources (HR). Think about all of the other areas of the company that this single strategic decision would have also impacted.

Helping you visualize all of the potential effects of your proposed change is what the Change Ripple Worksheet is for. It helps you build the dialogue with your group in order to answer the question:

• What other changes will be caused?

Each ripple going out from your intended change is potentially another complete change initiative (or project) that someone will likely need to plan and lead in order for your change effort to be successful. Alternatively, you may need to expand the scope of your change initiative to encompass one or more of the change ripples that you feel have the potential to make your primary change initiative fail.

Summary

In this chapter we looked at the fact that there are inevitably negative outcomes and risks that must be measured, mitigated, and managed in every change initiative. We also looked at some of the unexpected consequences of change and the risks and negative outcomes that you may encounter.

We looked at the three questions highlighted in the Negative Impacts Worksheet (which can be used for known negative outcomes and those negative impacts that might arise if a risk is realized).

1. Who is affected?
2. How are they affected?
3. Mitigation strategies

And we looked at how the Risks Worksheet can help you capture and discuss the three main issues involved.

1. Probability of the risk occurring
2. The potential impact of the risk should it occur
3. Strategies for reducing the chances of the risk occurring
   a. The **Negative Impacts Worksheet** is for capturing ideas on how to mitigate the negative impacts you expect to occur

And finally we talked about the importance of visualizing all of the potential effects of your proposed change using the Change Ripple Worksheet and asking the question:

- What other changes will be caused?

Looking at the expected negative outcomes, the risks (and potential negative impacts), and the ripples your change effort will cause, openly and honestly, will have a profound effect on your chances of succeeding. Therefore, don't cut off the conversations prematurely. Make sure you draw out every potential risk, every possible negative outcome, and that the entire group understands the scope and scale of the impacts of your change initiative (or project) on the organization.

CHAPTER 11

Breaking It Down

"The best thing about the future is that it comes only one day at a time."—
Abraham Lincoln

One of the reasons change efforts fail (in addition to be being poorly defined or poorly supported) is that they are often too big. If you want to make your change effort successful, you must break it down into smaller change efforts than can be managed and executed more easily. In this way you will have the ever important quick wins that initiate the positive forward momentum on the road to eventual change success. The biggest challenge is to find the pace of change the organization can successfully absorb and maintain until the change initiative (or project) is complete.

The Pace of Change

For your change effort to be a success you need to find the appropriate pace of change. Finding the right pace of change is very similar to trying to fly an airplane: Go too slow and you will stall. Go too fast and you will face an increasing amount of resistance, potentially depleting your fuel faster than expected.

In many cases, using up the energy for change too fast may prevent you from reaching your intended destination. One other danger of trying to change too fast, especially if you are trying to run too many change initiatives (or projects) at the same time in the same areas of the company, is that you may run into issues of change saturation.

At the same time you must resist the attraction of the quick win. John P. Kotter and others have written extensively[1] about the power and importance of quick wins, but they can distract people from engaging in more comprehensive and collaborative change planning. Pursuing quick wins can also tempt leaders to exhibit negative management behaviors, including jumping to conclusions and overreacting at the first sign of resistance.

The key for you as change leader is to identify a regular cadence for your change initiative (or project) that is comfortable for the organization as a whole. That cadence must be slow enough so that the incremental change can be readily adopted and absorbed but fast enough so that your positive forward momentum, executive sponsorship, and overall support are maintained. The pacing and the approach must ultimately help enlist the broader organization in the change effort by reducing feelings of uncertainty, reinforcing that the change is a team effort, and accumulating reasons to believe in the change outcomes and so that people choose change.

Building and Maintaining Momentum

There are many different reasons why people will do the right thing to help you build and maintain the momentum for your change initiative and to help you achieve sustained, collective momentum. The key to building and maintaining momentum is to understand and harness the different mind-sets that cause people to choose change; these include:

1. **Mover 'n' Shaker**
   - give these people the chance to be first
2. **Thrill Seeker**
   - these people like to try new things and experiment
3. **Mission-Driven**
   - these people need reasons to believe
4. **Action-Oriented**
   - these people just want to know what needs to be done
5. **Expert-Minded**
   - teach these people how to do it, and they will seek mastery
6. **Reward-Hungry**
   - these people want recognition for adopting the change
7. **Team Player**
   - these people are happy to help if you show them why the change will be helpful
8. **Teacher**
   - show these people how to get others to choose change

If you read through this list and imagine what might happen if you don't address any of these mind-sets in your plan, you should quickly find yourself with eight potential explanations for why people may be resisting your change effort. If any of these are playing out in the negative, then you must try and identify ways to turn these individuals back toward the positive as you work through the different phases of change.

The Phases of Change

You'll notice very quickly that I am focusing on having only three phases of change. Some people may argue that three is too few and elect to have more than three major phases for their change effort. If it works better for your organization to have more than three phases to your change effort, do it. I chose to target the three phases of change shown in figure 11.1 for the Change Phases Worksheet based on what you see in a circus.

If you look at how a traveling circus gets its work done, there are three phases:

1. setup and promotions (aka start-up)
2. performances (aka execution/empowerment)
3. tearing down, packing up, and relocating (aka wrap-up)

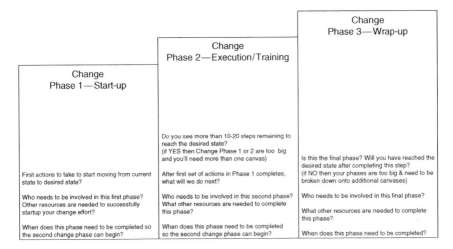

Figure 11.1 Change Phases Worksheet

And what is more fun and more similar to a change effort than a circus?

Let's now look at each of the three phases in turn and some questions to consider for each:

Change Phase 1: Start-up

The start-up phase is all about breaking inertia. The change planning process lives here. In this phase you will begin identifying the best people to become part of your change planning team; ideally, you will look at the Eleven Change Roles™ for guidance and build in some level of cross-functional perspectives and other sources of thought diversity. Intentionally striking that delicate balance between familiarity and diversity will improve the quality of your planning outcomes. Those outcomes will include creating your Change Planning Canvas™ and working through the other worksheets and tools in the toolkit.

Some of the questions you will want to discuss with your change planning team include the following:

1. What are the first actions we should take to begin moving from current state to desired state?
2. Who else needs to be involved in this first phase?
3. What other resources are needed to successfully start this change effort?
4. What resources do we need to line up in advance of our session to complete the Change Planning Canvas™? When should we hold this session?
5. When does this phase need to be completed so the second phase of the change can begin?
6. Do we have the level of executive sponsorship we will need for this change effort (or project) to be successful?

At the end of this first phase you should have a completed set of toolkit worksheets and a complete, vetted, and agreed upon Change Planning Canvas™ that you are ready to reproduce and post on walls around the company (where appropriate).

The completed worksheets and Change Planning Canvas™ will serve as the raw material for the creation of a more detailed set of change execution plans.

Change Phase 2: Execution/Empowerment

To begin the execution and empowerment phase, you will pass the baton of control of the change effort (or project) from the change planning team to your change execution (and empowerment) team. This latter team may have some different members, but ideally the teams will largely have the same members. In a well-executed change planning process, those individuals who are part of your change execution team but weren't part of your core change planning team will at least have been consulted during the planning process and will have been involved in the crafting of your change execution plans.

Some of the questions you will want to discuss with your change execution team include the following:

1. Has any new information emerged since the Change Planning Canvas™ was created that should lead to changes in the canvas or any of its associated execution plans?
2. Do we have someone in place to lead and manage the execution of each of the execution plans?
3. Do we have the right people on our change execution team?
4. Are we lacking any resources we need to begin the execution of our change effort?
5. What is the regular cadence (your pace of completing a piece of work) the organization is capable of absorbing and have we segmented the work so that each piece can be completed in the time allotted?
6. Do you see more than 10–20 work cycles occurring in your cadence to reach the desired state?
   a. If yes, then your change may be too big to execute in a single phase, and you'll need more than one canvas, one for each phase.
7. Has another change effort (or project) entered the execution phase that might jeopardize our ability to successfully execute our change plan if we start now (because of crucial overlapping resource needs)?
8. When does this phase need to be completed so the third change phase can begin?

It is during this execution phase that many organizations will choose to have a change management professional deal with the people aspects of the change and a project management professional handling the technical aspects of the change.

If you do a good job in setting up and planning your change using the Change Planning Toolkit™ and have a collaborative planning session to populate your Change Planning Canvas™ and to turn all of the outputs into a series of more detailed change plans, then you should be able to collaborate with a project manager and your change planning team to create an appropriate work breakdown structure (WBS). You will then be able to identify the scope and duration of different tasks you need to complete to achieve the goals of your change initiative (or project).

During this execution phase you will also want to focus on empowering those affected by the change with the new knowledge and skills they will need to have to carry out the new behaviors that will make the change a success. In most organizations, this will typically involve working with the training department to design educational experiences that will facilitate the behavioral changes necessary to support the change initiative and to make people transfer their feelings of mastery from the old way of doing things to the new way; this will remove a potentially major source of employee resistance to the change.

Finally, as you work to create the timelines for the execution (and empowerment) phase of your change initiative, you should be able to identify the point at which it will make sense to exit the execution phase and enter the wrap-up phase.

Change Phase 3: Wrap-up

Is this the final phase? Will you have reached the desired state after completing this step? If your answer is no, then your next cycle of change should be in the execution phase, and you will want to rethink what should be part of your wrap-up phase.

The wrap-up phase is all about tying up loose ends. This could include planning and executing the decommissioning of the system you're replacing (in the case of a systems implementation project) or making sure that all relevant websites or other documentation have any references to old procedures, processes, or organization names removed in order to fully transition to the new way of doing things (in the case of a change effort). Some of the questions you will want to discuss with your change wrap-up team include the following:

1. Has the change been effectively planned, fully executed, and successfully adopted?
2. If the change has been successfully made, what is left to do?
3. Who needs to be involved in this final phase?
4. What other resources are needed to complete this phase?
5. When does this phase need to be completed?

Doing good work during the setup phase using the toolkit will give you a strong set of plans to expedite the execution phase and leave you with a clearer picture of what remains to be done during the wrap-up phase so that the goals of your change initiative (or project) can be achieved.

It is during this wrap-up phase that many organizations fail to effectively cement the change, reinforce behaviors, and burn the bridges that might allow people to return to doing things the old way. In the wrap-up phase you should focus on checking that you've done everything possible to ensure adoption of and commitment to maintaining your intended change.

Your employees should be using their new knowledge and skills, and if they do not, this is your opportunity to remediate any lack of adoption or lingering resistance.

Finally, as you work to wrap up your project or change effort, you should make sure that you are getting measurements showing that you have met (or will soon meet) the goals of the change effort (or project) that were specified in the setup phase.

Summary

In this chapter we looked at the importance of breaking down any change effort into even smaller change efforts than can be managed and executed more easily, thus providing quick wins for forward momentum. We also looked at the challenge of finding the pace of change the organization can successfully maintain until the change initiative (or project) is complete.

We also discussed the different reasons why people will do the right thing to help you build and maintain the momentum for your change initiative, and why they may resist. In addition, we looked at the three main phases of change: start-up, execution/empowerment, and wrap-up.

We also looked at the questions you'll want to discuss with your change planning team in each phase using the Change Planning Toolkit™, and how you can be successful in each of the three phases.

CHAPTER 12

Now What (The Resource Challenge)

"Start by doing what's necessary, then do what's possible, and suddenly you are doing the impossible."—St. Francis of Assisi

As you plan your change effort, you will need to identify all of the human, capital, and other resources that will be required to successfully complete the change effort. You must also evaluate which of the resources required for success you already control and have available to allocate to this change effort, which resources you will need to acquire, and who controls the resources or has access to the resources you will need to make your change effort a success. At the same time you must evaluate the overall change saturation of both key individuals and the organization to determine a key component of the change readiness of the organization.

Change Saturation

When an organization's capacity for change absorption is exceeded by its pace of change, then that organization has reached a point of change saturation. The same is true for individuals, and ultimately an organization is a collection of individuals. The point of change saturation for organizations is typically achieved when one or more key individuals in the organization become saturated.

So ask yourself whether there are any employees currently involved in more change projects than they can productively participate in. To answer this question you must find a way to visualize the relative change saturation of different parts of the organization (ideally down to the level of the work team or individual). You'll need to map your organization and document the impacts on individuals across the organization. There are many different ways to do this, but ultimately what you are creating is a heat map. There are even some online tools for doing this. But whether you use a spreadsheet, paper, or some kind of software as a service (SaaS) tool, you're still going to need data for each individual affected for every change effort (or project) that is either currently underway or planned for implementation.

As part of your examination of change readiness, you'll need to identify for every new change effort where the hot spots are in your organization. And you must figure out how to best slot change efforts on your calendar so as to not overwhelm your staff or successful behavior change and the positive project outcomes will be jeopardized. In addition, you have to decide on potential strategies for moving day-to-day responsibilities from employees overburdened by your change effort to other staff members or use another employee in your change effort in their place.

Failure to identify where change saturation is already occurring or likely to occur, and planning a strategy to cope with saturation will result in delays and loss of momentum in your change effort, and this could cause the change effort not to achieve the desired positive outcomes.

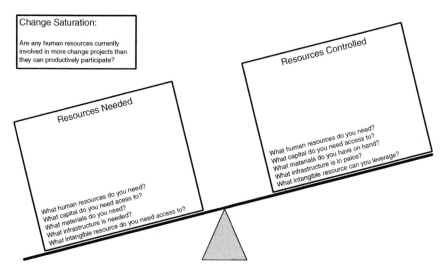

Figure 12.1 Resources and Change Saturation Worksheet

Sizing Up Your Resource Challenges

As your change planning team contemplates which required resources the change leadership team may already control, here are some the questions you and your team should discuss:

1. What human resources do we have?
2. What capital do we have access to?
3. What materials do we have on hand?
4. What infrastructure is in place?
5. What intangible resources can we leverage?

You'll notice that I draw a distinction between the change planning team and the change leadership team. This is because the team that plans the change isn't always the team that will continue on to see the change effort successfully implemented and reinforced in the organization.

The Resources and Change Saturation Worksheet (see figure 12.1) from the Change Planning Toolkit™ can be a great help here.

After identifying the resources the change leadership team already controls, the change planning team should identify the resources that are needed to make the change effort a success but are not currently controlled by the change leadership team. In the process you and the team should discuss a set of questions very similar to those above:

1. What human resources do we need?
2. What capital do we need access to?

3. What materials do we need?
4. What infrastructure is needed?
5. What intangible resources do we need access to?

It goes without saying that it is not enough to identify the resources the change leadership team will need but doesn't control. The change planning team must also work with the change leadership team on a plan to acquire control of the necessary resources or to work around not having those resources while still meeting the goals of the change effort.

Keep in mind, the first group of resources you will have to convince people to part with are the people who will form the change planning team. Depending on the size of the change effort, this group of people may be unable to still complete all of their normal work and their managers may need to identify other individuals to step in and complete their normal work while they plan the change effort.

Change as an Investment

If we look back at **The Eleven Change Roles**™ presented in chapter 2, there are several roles that will play an important part in the acquisition of the resources necessary to make your effort a success. Keep in mind that every change initiative is somewhat similar to raising money for a startup. Your **Change Planning Canvas**™ is like your business plan. It will help you keep your team focused when working with your Connectors because the latter know where the overt and hidden resources lie in the organization, and they have the personal connections and influence necessary to attract needed connections *and* access to resources.

Resource Controllers/Investors who have things you need—whether human resources, information resources, physical resources—need to be convinced to invest those resources in helping you successfully achieve your desired change. That is, you must have a very clear picture of how to appeal to the motivations, whether enlightened self-interest or dedication to the greater good, of the resource Controllers/Investors by working with your Evangelists/Supporters to tell a clear story about the advantages of the desired future state over the current state, a story that convinces them that the disruption of making the change is worth it.

Working with the Evangelists/Supporters will help you build a clear vision and create themes that weave seamlessly into your story as well as symbols that reinforce your vision and story and show the team's commitment to realizing the change effort's goals. Without these, you will find it hard to help potential resource investors understand or support the change goals. Thus, work with your evangelists/supporters to build what you'll need to break resource blockades.

Endorsers/Supporters can be another powerful force against resource blockades by helping you communicate the benefits of the change effort, despite the fact that they have no active role in pushing toward completion. Don't be afraid to reach out and ask for this assistance, but be sure to provide these individuals with the themes, symbols, and stories that you plan to use to reinforce the change vision and sustain the change effort's momentum.

Finally, you will want to activate your Influencers because they are a well-respected and forceful group in the organization; while they may lack the formal position of power of Sponsors/Authority Figures, they can still help rally people to the cause with their words and actions.

Bringing Creativity to the Resource Challenge

Creativity has a role to play in nearly all business activities, and working on overcoming resource constraints is one of the best places to harness people's creativity. "Think out of the box" is a meaningless and overused phrase. There is always a box, and it can be more powerful to use the "box" as a creative asset. Challenge your team members to use their creativity to think *inside the box*. Ask all participants:

1. If not now, when? We may not be able to get control of this resource now, but is there anything we can do early on in our change effort that might turn the no into a yes?
2. What would convince the resource controller that our change effort is a higher priority than what the resource is allocated to now?
3. How could we possibly achieve our goals if we never get access to this resource?
4. What are the substitutes for this resource?
5. What other resources could possibly provide 80 percent of what we need instead of 100 percent?
6. Have we done our best job of communicating the change effort's value?
7. What does the resource controller value? Do we have that? Or can we trade for it and then broker a deal?

Additional Ways to Fight Resource Constraints

It may not have been the focus of the bestselling business book *Blue Ocean Strategy*[1] by W. Chan Kim and Renee Mauborgne, but I learned several things from it that are good to keep in mind when it comes to battling resource constraints. Working through the Change Planning Canvas™ will help you identify several potential resource constraint solutions if you keep the following ideas in mind:

1. The Pareto Principle

In general, 80 percent of the positive outcomes in an organization come from an investment of 20 percent of the organization's resources, and 20 percent of the positive outcomes require 80 percent of the firm's resources. Look for opportunities to shift resources from cold spots to hot spots when you can.

2. Resource Trading

In any organization, you will occasionally find that another group has too much of something that you have too little of; in that case find something you can trade them.

3. Make It Real

Sometimes you don't get the resources you need because you haven't done a good enough job convincing people, of telling your story, of evangelizing. Build a crude prototype, draw a picture, find some way to show people how the change will benefit them and/or the organization. Don't just tell them.

Summary

In this chapter we looked at the role of human, capital, and other required resources in successfully completing the change effort. We considered that employees can become overburdened and that it is necessary to plan for their availability. We discussed the importance of evaluating which of the required resources we already control, which resources we will need to acquire, and who controls the resources we will need to make our change effort a success.

We looked at change saturation and its effects, some ways to track it, and some ideas for overcoming it. We viewed change as an investment, investigated different ways you can fight through resource resistance or to find a way around it. We also looked at questions you can use together with the Resources and Change Saturation Worksheet from the Change Planning Toolkit™.

Guest Expert

Beth Montag-Schmaltz (@bethmschmaltz)

Founding partner at PeopleFirm, a strategy and implementation consulting company that designs and implements solutions to address today's workforce challenges.

At PeopleFirm we don't believe in cookie-cutter solutions; yet, our clients benefit from our years of business experience, knowledge, and thought leadership. We do believe in taking a strategic approach and driving measureable value. We believe in straight talk and active leadership engagement. Most important, we believe that Your People = Your Success.

www.PeopleFirm.com

Bracing for the Next Wave of Change

A conflict is brewing between a veritable tsunami of change and the day-to-day work that shapes each employee's experience. It matters because the ever-increasing intensity of change is driving a surge of disengagement that we call *change fatigue*. This is caused by the pressure and frustrations of taking on simultaneous changes without adequate preparation. And when change fatigue gets the better of individuals and teams, the adoption of new initiatives plummets as the people most affected find their capacity to adapt diminished. The question, of course, is what to do about it.

First, let's back up a little. What "tsunami of change" am I talking about? As far back as 2010, the CEOs of major companies were already worried about change. In an IBM study,[1] these CEOs responded that they expected the amount of change in their organizations to continue to increase. In fact, the CEOs reported that coping with change is their most pressing challenge, especially because they also understood that their teams' capacity to manage the escalating volume of change was not keeping pace. Nearly 50 percent of CEOs surveyed said they lacked confidence in their organization's ability to manage the changes they will face. This is nothing new (change has been the top concern for global CEOs since 2004), and unfortunately nothing has changed. Other studies of executives are just as worrying: 48 percent of executives are not confident that their culture can quickly mobilize to serve new markets and customers; 50 percent indicate their culture is not adaptive enough to respond positively to change, and 44 percent are not sure their workforce is prepared to adapt to and manage change.[2]

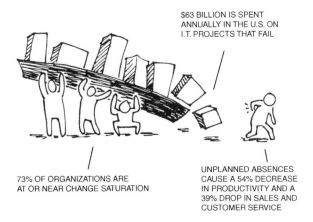

Figure 12.1.1 Three Painful Change Facts

Sources: Marsh survey on health, productivity and absenteeism—Prosci, 2009
Best Practices in Change Management and benchmarking study—CIO Insight, 2010

While organizations are marginally improving their capacity to effectively manage change, the volume, complexity, and magnitude of the changes to be absorbed are increasing at an unprecedented pace. Organizations just can't keep up. In fact, most companies continue to struggle to manage just the change created by large-scale projects, before even considering building real change capability across their enterprise (see figure 12.1.1).

Making matters more complicated, 77 percent of organizations surveyed by Prosci in 2013 reported that they are near or at the point of change saturation—the maximum amount of change their organization can absorb. This saturation dynamic, combined with the volume and speed of change, is resulting in unprecedented employee disengagement and resistance. Worse yet, as employees disengage, we are seeing a corresponding increase in project failures and an overall decrease in organizational productivity as well as higher employee turnover, dissatisfaction, and absenteeism—all these are effects of increasing change fatigue.

Your Brain on Change

So why is it that people resist change? Neuroscience tells us that the answer may lie in the way our brains work. In his first book, *Emotional Intelligence*, Daniel Goleman[3] coined the term "amygdala hijack" as a way of describing how the emotional part of the brain (the amygdala) regulates the fight-or-flight response—and how it can make us respond irrationally when we feel threatened. The path to the amygdala is faster than the path to our cerebral cortex (which houses our rational and logical thoughts). When a rush of stress hormones floods the body, the amygdala takes over before the cerebral cortex can weigh in. And change triggers the release of stress hormones in our bodies.

But the problem goes beyond pure brain chemistry. A talent management study conducted by Towers Watson tells us two things we already pretty much knew: that employees are working harder than ever today and that they are suffering from change fatigue.[4] But why the connection between the two? Well, we are all asking our employees to do more with less. This means we need our employees to multitask more than ever and to constantly prioritize which items in their day-to-day job will have the greatest impact on the organization. This would be fine, except for one major issue: neurological studies show that multitasking just doesn't work.

The cofounder and COO of Buffer, Leo Widrich, states: "The problem with multitasking is that we're splitting our brain's resources. We're giving less attention to each task, and probably performing worse on all of them: When the brain tries to do two things at once, it divides and conquers, dedicating one-half of our gray matter to each task."[5]

The book *Brain Rules* by John Medina also discusses multitasking. Medina writes that research shows individuals' error rate goes up by 50 percent and they take twice as long to get work done when they are attempting to multitask.[6]

With this in mind, we need to ask ourselves: are we requiring our people to do too much and creating unintended consequences in doing so? What happens when we add the stress of change pressure to brains already on overdrive from trying to do too much at once? And just how much can employees take on at once?

So What Do You Do about All This?

First, you need to get a handle on the change you are currently experiencing. If you don't have insight into the change portfolio at your organization, don't worry, you're not the only one. Today most organizations lack a current and complete inventory of the change occurring across their business units. Over 60 percent of companies report having no structured process to manage their portfolio of change. Even more organizations report that their course of action is to "do nothing" to mitigate the risks of change saturation.[7]

Don't Join the "Do-Nothing" Crowd.

I suggest taking a small, yet significant step by surveying what large, cross-functional initiatives your organization is planning to deploy within the next 12 months. Then understand which stakeholders are most affected by these initiatives. The areas where those intersect are what we like to call "change collisions"—that is, changes occurring at the same time to the same stakeholders and ultimately competing for the mental capacity of already overloaded employees. These are the initiatives that will almost always end up crashing and burning, either upon deployment or within the first three months of implementation.

Once you have this insight, work with your leadership to consider avoiding these collisions. Bring your teams alternatives. And remember, while executives never like to hear the word "stop," this information may convince them of the wisdom of altering their course to mitigate the risk of expensive and costly project failures. Just consider this statistic: *$63 billion* is spent in the United States annually on IT projects that *fail*.[8] That's enough to get any executive's attention.

Here are a few more ideas for reducing change fatigue:

- *Adapt:* Alter the deployment timing of your effort to maximize the best possible timing for adoption.
- *Adjust:* Is there anything in the "rhythm of the business" that can be changed—delayed, removed, or scaled back?
- *Integrate:* Should the change initiatives concerning certain stakeholder groups be consolidated—that is, should communication and training efforts be rolled into one?
- *Shift:* Should one project go before the other to mitigate change saturation?
- *Intervene:* What intervention should be applied to mitigate the risk of change saturation? More resources added to the project? Additional change management activities to ensure readiness?

Building Change Capability

Agile, innovative, responsive, nimble, creative, flexible…this is how we describe the organizations that will succeed in today's business environment. We all know what we're aiming for. The irony is that not everyone realizes that those words also describe a change-capable organization—that the two are, in fact, one and the same thing. Organizations that successfully embed change capability into the fabric of the company will develop a competitive advantage in their markets. I can't state it strongly enough: *responsiveness to change = competitive advantage.* "An agile organization has more strategic insight into human capital strategy and the workforce capabilities needed to execute strategy rapidly and effectively."[9]

Of course, building real change capability into an organization isn't easy. But it's not impossible. Building a strong foundation for change, along with a common taxonomony, is the first and most critical step. As a change leader, you will also need to select (or create) a change framework that fits with your organization's culture and values. At PeopleFirm, we use the following framework, which focuses on growing resilient change capabilities and cultivating a disciplined approach to change (see figure 12.1.2).

From there, you can take multiple paths depending on the maturity of your organization. If you have a culture of strong rigor in project management, it may make sense to focus on aligning change activities into specific projects and critical organizational governance processes. In this case it likely also makes sense to ensure that your organization has in-house expertise, such as a change center of excellence (CoE) or change management office (CMO). These institutions will prove their worth almost at once with more successful project implementations.

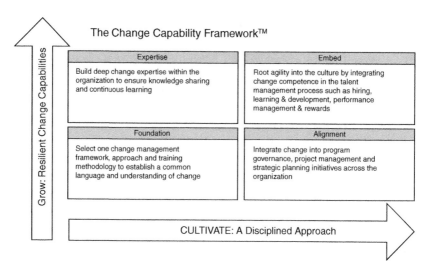

Figure 12.1.2 The Change Capability Framework

But while building a foundation, aligning to critical business functions, and ensuring internal expertise are all important, the true secret to building up change capability lies in your talent management processes. If your organization can build the muscle to source and hire, promote, train, develop, incent, and recognize effective change behaviors, you will start changing the nature of change in your organization.

What I mean is this: what would happen if instead of focusing on projects, you worked to nurture change-embracing behavior across the entire organization, at all times? Let's examine the typical technology startup, since companies like that are well known for the kind of organizational agility we're looking for. Their normal operation mode—at all times, not just around specific projects—is to embrace and successfully adjust to change. In fact, change capability is systemic throughout such companies and is actually a necessary part of the skillset of each employee.

In other words, to achieve a high level of business agility, the ability to successfully manage and respond to change is built into the very structure of the company, including at the level of each employee's skills. This means that as change continually presents itself—whether in response to a new competitor, growth, new IT systems, or a wide variety of other business stressors—the startup company and its employees are well equipped to keep the company on its trajectory of growth.

The ten thousand dollar question then is: can you apply this to your organization? I think you can. The key is applying the lessons of the nimble startup company to how you build your people programs. Instead of purely relying on a central CMO or CoE tasked with helping large projects manage change successfully, think about the following guidelines to take your approach to change to the next level.

Six ways to embed change behavior into the very fabric of your organization:

1. Equip leaders and employees with solid change skills and make those skills part of competency training.
2. Work change principles into job descriptions and hiring guidelines in order to hire change-capable employees.
3. Put change language in value statements in order to communicate clearly to the organization the importance of being a change-agile employee.
4. Work change principles into employee goal setting and reward and recognize change-ready behavior.
5. Train people to recognize when they are resisting change and teach, motivate, and reward them to self-correct.
6. Communicate clearly and regularly about how employees contribute to the organization's success and strategic goals; make sure they know their effort matters.

In other words, all employees should instinctively work in a change-capable manner at all times; how they think, act, and react should reflect solid change principles. This way you'll be building a nimble culture of change capability, and agility will become the "new normal."

What are those key change principles that you should base your nimble culture on Employees capable of change will be able to do the following:

- *Seek to understand first:* They will actively seek information about new work situations and strive to understand the rationale and implications for changes in work responsibilities or the environment in general.
- *Self-diagnose:* They will understand when they are exhibiting what looks like resistance—and will stop, pause, and determine a better path forward.
- *Approach with cautious optimism:* They will treat change and new situations as opportunities for learning or growth, identify the benefits of the changes, and speak positively about the change to others.
- *Manage themselves through the change:* They will develop appropriate strategies when needed to alter conditions that create stress and to sustain physical and mental health during the change.

In Summary

How do we know how much change is too much? There is no empirical study that I can point to that defines the point of saturation. Instead, look at your organization's history of successful change. How much else was competing for your employee's attention during those initiatives? Are there certain groups within your organization that typically are more resilient than others? This concept of a *change threshold* will vary from one organization to the next as well as within an organization's business units or departments, but it is important to be aware of and watch for this threshold. Remember, with our "multitasking myth" in mind, we have to ask ourselves how much randomization we're throwing at employees and set limits as to how much change is too much.

Imagine a day when instead of demonstrating immediate resistance, employees understood how to handle change and knew that their performance was dependent on how well they responded to new initiatives. And what if middle managers were to remember the change training that outlined their critical role in successful change and would apply that learning when change gets tough? Or envision an organization where change sponsorship is not something that has to be justified but is an expected part of what leadership is all about. Sound good?

By proactively managing change saturation and building a change-capable, agile organization, this vision can be your reality. With attention, your organization over time can exercise the necessary change muscles to take on more and more change and still remain successful. This is a must, considering that tsunami of change that's on the horizon.

CHAPTER 13

Building the Case for Change

"The secret of change is to focus all of your energy, not on fighting the old, but on building the new."—Socrates

Change is difficult for organizations and individuals, and they often seek to avoid it. It can be difficult to convince people that change is needed. It is up to the leaders of an organization and the change planning team to make the case for change. Change requires actively selling people on the merits and benefits of each change effort and to rally their logical, emotional, and political support for the change initiative.

As you begin to craft a strategy for shifting people from the current state to the desired state, keep in mind Smith and Connors' "Case for Change Best Practices":[1]

1. Make it real.
2. Make it applicable to your audience.
3. Make it simple and repeatable.
4. Make it convincing.
5. Make it a dialogue.

Telling Your Change Story

A recent McKinsey & Company study[2] found that organizations whose senior management teams communicated openly throughout their organization about a transformation's progress and success were eight times more likely to succeed than those who did not. Leaders using a consistent change story to align the organization with their transformation's goals were nearly four times more likely to be successful as those who did not. There are several points for leaders to include as part of their efforts to build the case for change. Leaders must include in their change stories descriptions for the following:

1. The context that establishes why changes are needed now
   - Include external drivers (threats) and internal drivers (opportunities)
   - What does the organization stand to gain by making the change?
2. What will change and what won't
   - Personalize the change for the individual
3. The process and timeline for implementing the proposed changes
   - What is the implementation going to look like?
4. The expected change benefits
   - Document the change at multiple levels: company, department, and individual
5. The consequences of delaying change or moving slowly
   - What does the organization stand to lose if it doesn't make the change quickly?

6. The expectations of your stakeholders
   - How will we measure the progress of the change effort?
   - What are the goals for the change effort?
   - How will we measure whether the change effort is successful or not?
7. Commitments required from senior leaders
   - What level of support does this change effort enjoy?
   - What access to resources will this change effort have?

Remember, you are building the case for change and must establish a baseline level of awareness, understanding, and support for the changes.

At the same time you are helping people envision what the changes will mean for them, the roles they might play in facilitating and cementing the changes, and what they can expect as the change effort moves toward successful implementation.

Making the case for change is often very similar to making the case for an innovation. You must first understand and sell the problems before you can build and sell the solutions. And because change comes as the result of a sustained effort to achieve a set of specific outcomes that include some behavior changes, identifying the outcomes and behavior changes you are looking to achieve and defining how you will measure their attainment is key.

Changing Outcomes, Changing Behavior

When engaging in a change effort, it is important to focus not on outputs but on outcomes. The difference between them is subtle but outputs are usually activity-based and outcomes are behavior-based.

There are several good behavior modification frameworks out there including the Six Boxes framework[3] from Carl Binder, the *Six Sources of Influence*[4] framework from VitalSmarts, and the Results Pyramid[5] from Partners in Leadership that start with the desired performance changes, results, or outcome shifts and work backward.

Change at the organizational level happens after change happens at the individual level. Therefore, personal change frameworks like these can help you look at changing organizational behavior one individual at a time. Consider the following as you look at the change from the perspective of the individual:

1. Teach people the new skills necessary to be successful at the new way of doing things.
2. Break up the learning into short intervals where you can give people immediate feedback.
3. Prepare for people to have regressions back to the current status quo.
4. Identify the moments when people will be most tempted to regress to the current status quo.
5. Create strategies that reinforce the new way of doing things.

6. Change the physical environment to support the change.
7. Consider the social connections in the organization and look for influential individuals who can help accelerate the change process.
8. Use vivid storytelling to help reinforce that the change is desirable.
9. Find ways for people to feel what the new change might be like.
10. Seek to understand individuals' motivations and apply the use of carrots and sticks (or withholding of carrots) strategically.

Planning to Spread

When we are building the case for change, we are building the case for a collection of ideas, and we are hoping that these ideas will go viral.

We've all seen the viral videos that seemingly come out of nowhere and garner millions of views on YouTube. Whether we work in marketing, change management, or some other part of the organization, we are always selling ideas, and for an idea to spread, one thing is required:

- Resonance

Resonance can be very difficult to achieve because it is affected by many factors, including:

- the message itself
- message visualization
- timing
- societal trends
- reinforcement by independent voices
- and many more factors

When adopting an idea into their new pattern of behavior people move through three stages:

- awareness
- trial
- repeat

With most ideas, whether they are commercialized into a product or are intended to be something less tangible, most people either don't even reach the first stage (awareness) or progress past it to trial. If an idea fails to resonate, then people move on to try other ideas they become aware of or return to their previous status quo.

But ideas that resonate drive people to repeat their new behavior and add this new idea to their regular behavior patterns. Those individuals will then also help to create awareness of the idea in other people and increase the likelihood that these others will move to the trial stage. Resonance makes an idea spreadable.

And your success is often determined by whether you can get your ideas to spread.

This is true whether we are talking about an IT project, a Six Sigma continuous improvement effort, a change initiative, a Lean event, a marketing campaign, or a project commercializing an invention into a potential innovation. And while spreadability can't be guaranteed, an idea can be built to spread.

In figure 13.1 you'll find a simple framework that can help you think through how you might help an idea to spread. It's based on the same principles as mind mapping, and it will help you start with a particular node in mind (someone you'd like to reach and influence) and work backward, identifying how to evolve your idea to best reach and influence that particular node. Or you can work from the idea outward and focus primarily on the *who* and the *why*.

The key questions to consider as you are planning to spread your idea are the following:

- What is your idea or message? (Does it resonate with your target audience?)
- Who are you trying to reach?
- How will you reach them?
- When will they be most receptive to the message or idea?
- Where will they be most receptive to the message or idea?
- Why will they engage? (What value will they get?)
- Why will they share? (What value will they derive?)
- How will they share?

Working your way thoughtfully through these questions will increase the chances that your idea will spread, but there are no guarantees. Going through the process, however, will help you refine your idea, help you think through the mechanics of how you might encourage engagement, and it may even help you uncover flaws in your idea that you missed before.

Measuring Success

One of the most important parts of looking at the potential benefits, discussing them, and even ranking them on their importance and impact is creating a collection of goals and metrics that coalesce into expected change outcomes. These expected change outcomes should reflect the primary benefits you must achieve, and it should be clear how you will know when you have achieved these benefits of the change effort (or project).

To help you outline your goals and success measures for your change initiative, I have included several worksheets in my Change Planning Toolkit™ that take a Goal Question Metric (GQM) approach for goal and metric creation; they use an

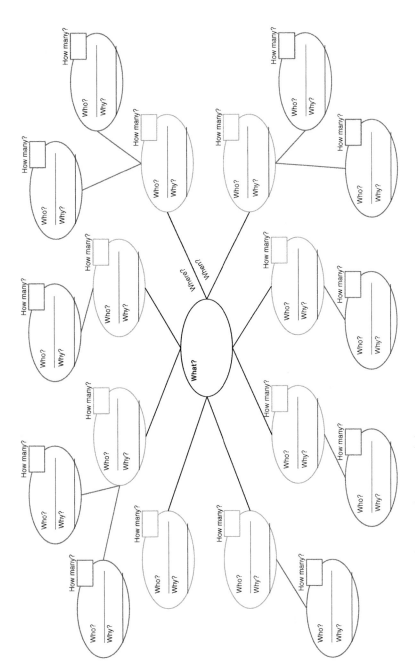

Figure 13.1 Spreading the Change Worksheet

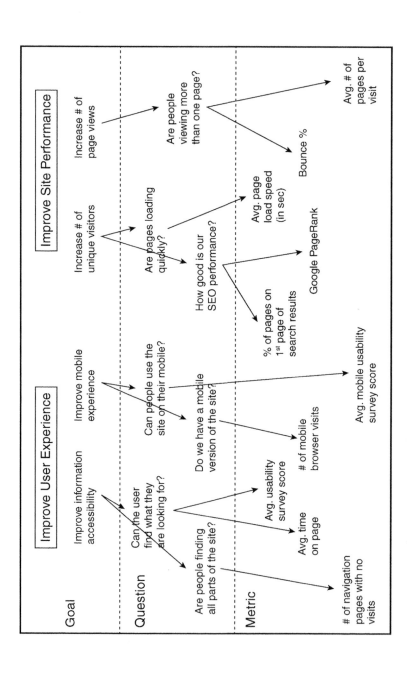

Figure 13.2 Defining Metrics with the Goals in Mind

example from a web redesign project (see figure 13.2). Buyers of the toolkit will find that these worksheets help identify the goals and metrics to track during the change initiative (or project) at various intervals.

Ultimately, your measurement activities should help you track and communicate the progress you are making toward your expected change outcomes.

Summary

In this chapter we first discussed the importance of creating a clear and compelling story and then consistently telling that same story as you build your case for change. A good story should include:

1. The context that establishes why changes are needed now
2. What will change and what will not
3. The process and timeline for implementing the proposed changes
4. The expected change benefits
5. The consequences of delaying change or moving slowly
6. The expectations of your stakeholders
7. Commitments required from senior leaders

Always remember that you must first understand and sell the problems before you can build and sell the solutions.

We spoke about the importance of focusing not on outputs but on the expected outcomes for your change effort. We also looked at the role of behavior modification frameworks in helping to turn individual change into organizational change.

We then looked at what's involved in building an idea to spread and the stages people must go through to successfully adopt a new behavior.

Finally we discussed the importance of collaboratively defining, measuring, and communicating the goals, metrics, and expected outcomes of your change effort. When you focus on telling a good story, selling the problems before the solutions, understanding and influencing behavior change, and measuring and communicating the progress toward your expected change outcomes, you'll find that you can effectively build the case for change and increase your chances of successfully achieving it.

Guest Expert

Brett Clay, PhD (@sellingchange)

Founder and president of Change Leadership Group, LLC and author of *Selling Change: 101 Secrets for Growing Sales by Leading Change.*

www.ChangeLeadershipGroup.com

Selling Change

We likely all agree that one of the most difficult tasks a change agent faces is getting people to support a change initiative. Even if people don't actively resist the change and only adopt a strategy of passive inaction, that inaction could doom the initiative to fail in implementation.

Practitioners have been struggling with this challenge, and scholars have been studying it since before the days of the Greek philosopher Socrates, who received capital punishment for "corrupting" the youth by challenging the status quo. More recently, Harvard professor John Kotter has stressed the importance of developing a sense of urgency, saying: "The iceberg we're standing on is melting, and if we don't do something soon, we're going to drown!!" Other scholars have stressed the importance of establishing and reinforcing dissatisfaction with the current situation. Yet others emphasize the importance of painting a clear vision of a desirable future state. In the sales profession, salespeople are taught to identify a compelling event—one that will make the current situation unacceptably costly. The prospect of a melting iceberg, the entry of a new competitor, the end of the fiscal year, or events in the regulatory environment are examples of such events.

These ideas have one thing in common. They recognize the necessity that people have to "buy" the change. That is, people must make an affirmative decision to take action in support of the change or at least not to oppose it if the initiative is to be implemented successfully. Therefore, one role of a change agent is to "sell" the change to stakeholders.

But we need to be careful with how we conceptualize "selling." The concept of selling is often associated with persuasion and coercion. A great salesperson is often thought to be so persuasive that the salesperson could sell ice to Alaskan Eskimos and sunshine to Pacific Islanders. Steve Jobs's "reality distortion field" is the exemplar of charisma and persuasiveness. Alternatively, sales managers often look for "meat-eating bulldogs" that tenaciously and relentlessly chew away at obstacles until anyone or anything in the way of an affirmative decision finally surrenders. Again, Steve Jobs is an oft-cited example of a change agent who won't take no for an answer.

However, these approaches often don't work when selling a change initiative, and you might not be successful modeling yourself after Steve Jobs. Why? First, the change agent's job is not done when the initiative has been approved. The change agent must often rely on the stakeholders to implement the change. Steve Jobs could demand action because he could and did dole out punishments and rewards. But research, such as Edward Deci's self-determination theory[2], suggests that even if you think you have the power to punish and reward stakeholders, the change initiative will enjoy a much higher probability of success if the stakeholders "buy" the change for their own intrinsic reasons.

Imagine that you don't have the ability to reward or punish stakeholders. Imagine that they are like rebellious teenagers, unlikely to do anything you ask. For most of us, that isn't hard to imagine. That's the reality a change agent faces every day. So what to do? To make matters worse, imagine that the change you are selling isn't associated with an existential crisis for the organization. There isn't a melting iceberg. What then? How do you get people to take action?

I have found that people will take action only when they feel compelled by a force. If you've made the same observation, we're not alone. Social psychologist Kurt Lewin posited that very theory[3], which underlies the field of organizational development (OD). The task of the change agent, then, is to discover what forces stakeholders are feeling—and then to harness those forces to energize the change. Lewin called this process *force field analysis*. This analysis compares driving forces to resisting ones. While that analysis can be useful, it is a trivial subset of what Lewin meant. Actually, he used the metaphor of a field of tall grass, where each blade of grass is a different force the person feels. Force field analysis, in its full form, is the process of discovering the blades of grass in that field and seeking to understand how the person who feels them is influenced by them.

Lewin observed that forces can come from within the person (internal) or from the person's environment (external). I've found that managers, salespeople, and change agents tend to look only at a person's environment; then they classify those environmental forces as either drivers or resistors. They think they're done. But after nearly 30 years of practice, I've found that, as Deci has shown, people are moved more by internal forces than external ones.[4] If Deci's 40 years of academic research are not compelling enough, I'm here to tell you: the most successful salespeople don't use external motivations like persuasion and coercion. They find out what the person wants and why he or she wants it. In other words, they discover the internal forces the person is feeling. That's why a great salesperson's selling process looks effortless. The salesperson is like a jujitsu master harnessing the other person's energies and motivations.

In the sales profession, an important step in the sales process is called discovery. To aid me in the discovery of a person's internal forces, I found it helpful to divide the broad category of internal forces into three subcategories. The first and most important is the category of a person's internal needs. These include the familiar needs in Maslow's hierarchy, such as security, belonging, and esteem.[5] This category also includes needs such as personal values, ideals, and moods, and it can even include Freudian needs, such as narcissism or feelings of inferiority. I'm not suggesting you need to be a clinical psychologist to sell change successfully; however, you need to have the right attitude adjustment. Your attitude should be: people will do something because they want to do it, not because you or anything else is forcing them to do it. As Deci would say, people are "self-determined."[6] If you have that attitude, you'll be able to discover what a person wants. She or he will probably tell you if you ask.

The second category of forces is a person's behavioral tendencies—his or her personality and habits. People simply have different preferences, styles, and habits. Walking down the hall of an organization is like walking through a zoo where each person has different stripes, feathers, and antlers. Whenever possible, you'll want to adapt your strategies and tactics so they are congruent with stakeholders' tendencies. For example, if a person is analytically oriented, you can provide lots of data. If a person prefers to be a follower, perhaps having that person join a a coworker or a group would increase his or her comfort with—and support of—the change. Of course, there are as many different tactics as there are differences in people.

The last category of forces consists of the cognitive strategies a person employs to manage himself or herself. For example, People often use schedules, plans, and budgets to manage their behavior. They may also rely on others, such as group exercise classes, to provide "scaffolding" that supports their desired behaviors. What techniques are your stakeholders using? By the way, in an organizational context, companies employ project management methods, many financial planning processes, performance appraisal systems, and many other operational procedures to manage the organization's behavior. Keep in mind that from an individual's point of view, those are external, environmental forces. By being aware of stakeholders' cognitive strategies, you may discover ways to leverage the latter.

Taken together, these four forces—internal needs, behavioral tendencies, cognitive strategies, and environment—provide a checklist of things to be aware of when seeking to discover the whats and whyof stakeholders' wants.

One mistake I've seen over and over in my professional practice is that people often feel pressured to initiate a change quickly—even before each stakeholder has processed the forces he or she feels and made the emotional commitment to the change. However, every ounce of advance buy-in will save you pounds of pain and delay later. Taking extra time at the start to line up all the forces for each stakeholder will help maintain the momentum of the change initiative and overcome the challenges and setbacks that will inevitably occur in the implementation stages.

Let's summarize: Selling change is not a matter of charisma, persuasion, rewards, or punishments. It's about being a sincerely curious and active listener. Force field analysis is not about making sure the driving forces overwhelm the resistance. It's about discovering and harnessing the what and why that make stakeholders tick.

Go ahead and be enthusiastic, tenacious, and communicative. You're more likely to succeed that way than if you are hesitant, inconsistent, and difficult to understand. But if you also pair your urgency and tenacity with listening and you harness the forces of change, especially the internal forces, you will become a truly effective and efficient leader of change!

CHAPTER 14

Communicating Change

"For change to be human, people must choose to change."—Braden Kelley

When it comes to communicating change, too often managers rely on plain, boring text emails that nobody reads instead of treating change communications like a marketing campaign and using all of the same tools that the creative, strategy, and data/analytics teams at a marketing agency might use.

In chapter 6 we looked at picking the right change targets for your change efforts. There were three main questions for the change planning team to consider:

1. Who are we making this change for?
2. Who will feel the greatest change benefit?
3. Why should this person or group be the target?

As the change planning team considers the answers to these questions, it's important to consider another series of questions:

1. Why might people resist?
2. Why might people support the effort?
3. Where will people have concerns?
4. What transitions might people struggle most with?
5. What kinds of communications do we need to create to inform, convince, motivate, move, or inspire people?
6. How might we best help each individual in the group transition his or her behavior from the old way of doing things to the new?
7. And many others.

All of these questions are designed to aid in identifying potential change targets and to select a primary change target that will drive the successful achievement of the desired change outcomes.

Answering these questions helps companies choose a primary change target and facilitates segmentation of the change audience.

Communicating Change Should be Treated like a Marketing Activity

In many change efforts, the planning and execution of communications unfortunately often falls to a project manager instead of a communications specialist. While many change efforts are in fact projects, this doesn't mean that the project manager is best suited to plan and execute a communications strategy

"What if, and I know this sounds kooky,
we communicated with the employees."

Figure 14.1 Importance of Employee Communications

designed to transition people from their existing behaviors to new ones and to reinforce those new behaviors.

Well-trained project managers may understand the basics of crafting a status update email, maintaining, and communicating an issues log, and doing some basic stakeholder management communications. But to support a successful change initiative additional skills and expertise are needed, and this often means pulling in people from the corporate communications or marketing teams to aid the project manager (and change manager) in delivering the right content with the right messages at the right time to the right people using the right communication channels to facilitate and reinforce the behavior modifications necessary to achieve the desired change outcomes (see figure 14.1).

The person in charge of planning and executing the change communications must think like a marketer. This means focusing on the basics of marketing communications, including messaging, branding, channel selection, targeting and segmentation, and measurement. Marketers ask themselves questions such as the following:

1. Why is this communication important?
2. Who is the target audience for this communication?
3. What's the primary message of this particular communication?
4. Is this communication consistent with the brand essence of the change effort?
5. Is there a clear call to action?
6. What communication channels are most appropriate for this particular communication?
7. What contact strategy will best support the desired change outcomes?
8. What should the communications calendar and contact strategy look like (sequence, channel, timing, etc.)?
9. How do all of the communications work together?
10. How will we measure the performance of each individual communication?

This means that good communications are intentionally informed by insights about the people they are intended for, and using those insights to drive the creation of messages will ultimately help bridge the gap between the audience's existing mind-set and behaviors and the desired outcomes.

Crafting the Communications Strategy

The strategy for any series of communications you plan to execute in support of the necessary behavior modifications must incorporate several components, each aligned with your segmentation of the change audience. These components include:

- key messages
- symbols
- signals
- themes
- timing
- sequencing
- scheduling
- channel selection
- channel availability
- channel usage frequency
- competition or collaboration for channel access

The last component, tracking the campaign, is the most important of all. Marketers measure the performance of every marketing communication, so that they can refine the message and creative components and also so they can optimize other variables, such as day of the week, time of day, communication channel in which to send messages, etc. Campaign tracking includes success metrics (open rates, click rates, engagement metrics, return on marketing investment (ROMI), etc.). Marketers also look beyond Outlook emails to use a variety of different communication channels to best influence the desired behavior modifications.

Here is a list of potential communication channels to leverage:

- HTML emails with tracking
- posters
- desktop drops
- PC wallpaper
- PC screensaver
- voicemails
- text messages (SMS)
- mobile apps
- instant messages (IMs via Microsoft Communicator, Lync, Skype for business, etc.)

- articles on intranet
- corporate social media campaigns (Yammer, etc.)
- table tents in cafeteria
- table tents in conference rooms
- flyers in restroom stalls
- flyers on conference room doors
- flyers on building doors
- lawn signs around campus
- banners
- video messages on screens in building lobbies
- video messages on intranet
- video messages in email
- video broadcasts via Skype? Lync?
- brown bag information sessions
- Town hall meetings
- road show (visiting one department at a time)
- cascade approach (senior leaders informed, who then inform middle managers, who then inform front line supervisors, who then inform line staff)

Great Communications Require a Team

There is a reason why advertising and marketing agencies have creative *teams*, strategy *teams*, account *teams*, and so on (see figure 14.2). The reason is that when people with different backgrounds combine their different perspectives in support of a clearly defined desired outcome, they bring different knowledge and insights to bear in creating potential solutions that are informed by a combined understanding of the client, the customers, communications best practices, and artistic principles. When marketing and advertising teams work well, they have positive creative tension; they evolve promising idea fragments into strong, complete ideas that achieve resonance.

Figure 14.2   Great Communications Require a Team

Resonance is another key to successful change. When you achieve resonance with your primary change target and the other important groups of people from your change audience through your change communications, then you can more easily move groups of people toward your desired change outcomes.

Summary

In this chapter we explored what goes into the creation of a communications strategy; we saw that communicating change as a marketing activity can amplify the impact and effectiveness of your communications. We also looked at how great communications require a team and what can be gained from taking a more collaborative approach to change communications.

In addition, we took a look at a wide variety of different communication channels that we might leverage for change. We considered what treating change communications like a marketing activity might mean by asking ourselves a series of questions and by thinking about the role of messaging, branding, channel selection, targeting and segmentation, and measurement in building a successful communication strategy.

Guest Experts

Ty Montague (@tmontague) and Rosemarie Ryan (@RosemarieRyan)

Cofounders and CEOs of co:collective, a strategy and innovation company that works with leadership teams to conceive and execute innovation in the customer experience using a proprietary methodology called StoryDoing®.

www.cocollective.com

StoryDoing® and Organizational Change

Ben Horowitz famously said, "A company without a story is a company without a strategy.[1]" We couldn't agree more. Having a clear and distinctive story is critical in the bottom-up, transparent, socially dynamic business world today. However, there's a distinction to be made between broadcasting your story—storytelling—and living your story, or what we at co:collective, a strategy and innovation company, call StoryDoing®. In a world where actions speak louder than words, where what you do is more important than what you say, placing your story at the center of your business and organizing around it makes the difference between a good company and a great one.

Building a Great StoryDoing® Organization

1. Start with a Quest

There's nothing greater than the power of an idea to transform an organization. Great StoryDoing® companies are on a quest, one that *everyone* in the organization can rally around and adopt. A good quest defines an ambition for the business, beyond commercial aspiration; it captures the narrative and purpose of the brand. That kind of quest has an expansive view of the business in question and thus enables the people working there to challenge category norms and open up new options. A quest is a tool that people inside the organization use every day to make decisions and build the future.

Target's story is about democratizing style and elevating the everyday. The company is on a quest to make sure that everyone, regardless of budget, has access to fabulous style. The organization turned that quest into action by breaking the conventions of big box retailing and partnering with icons in the design and fashion world. By partnering with companies from Michael Graves to Liberty of London, Target proved that a champagne taste could be had on a beer budget.

2. StoryDoing® for the Organization Starts with the CEO

Employees will not fully commit to a quest until they sense the full support of leadership. Gary Hamel, in his book *The Future of Management*, says that "Today, no leader can afford to be indifferent to the challenge of engaging employees in the work of creating the future. Engagement may have been optional in the past, but it's the whole game today."[2]

One of the most famous story-doing CEOs is Steve Jobs. The story of Apple has been told through every action the company takes, from the breakthrough products to the visionary advertising. In addition to his obsession with world-changing products, Jobs famously spent two hours a week with his marketing partners looking at the concepts in development. He did not do this because he was a particular fan of advertising but because he considered everything that Apple makes, from iPhones to ads, a vital part of conveying the Apple story and therefore worthy of his personal attention. This is still rare behavior for a CEO today.

3. StoryDoing® Organizations Build Their Story into Their Culture

You can copy a product, but you can't copy culture. For example, Tony Hsieh founded Zappos on an audacious quest to deliver happiness. The key to making that story true was building a culture where making the customer happy was the ultimate metric of success. The old metric of just getting customers off the phone again as quickly as possible was replaced with the new one of keeping them on until they were truly satisfied. Building a relationship and rapport was as valued as making a sale. Traditional hierarchies were eliminated, and the folks on the phone were empowered to solve problems in real time without checking with the supervisor. To make sure of hiring people who could make that really happen, Zappos offered new hires four weeks after they had been hired as customer service representatives several thousand dollars to quit. Thanks to the company's belief in its employees and the importance of making customers happy, Zappos has become an $850 million business and has one of the happiest workforces in the country.

StoryDoing® organizations don't tell their story so much as live it. They express it through every action they take—from the products they make to the customer service they provide to the way they incentivize and reward their people. As a result, StoryDoing® companies are nimbler, more efficient, and tougher competitors than traditional storytelling companies.

4. StoryDoing® Companies Are Organized by Shared Purpose

Great StoryDoing® companies build their story into everything they do—these companies don't follow the latest consumer trends or try to outpace the known competition. Instead, such companies imagine their future based on their quest, a vision that becomes a blueprint for organizing the company.

Nike has been in the business of quest-led innovation for more than 50 years. It started out small, making shoes for people who loved to run, but its ambition was much bigger. Nike's quest is to bring inspiration and innovation to the athlete in all of us. That ambition has always framed and focused all of the company's innovation, from starting with technically superior athletic shoes and the famous waffle-tread shoe, to most recently expanding into the digital platform space with Nike+. Nike no longer just builds great shoes for runners; it builds and creates the software that enables runners—seven million worldwide—to track, measure, compare, and share their runs. This has demanded new capabilities, a digital sports division, and new investments in talent. These investments are made all in service of the company's quest, a quest that brought both focus and the freedom to expand outside its original product category.

In a world of finite resources, organizing your company's talent and resources around the quest of your business brings focus and helps separate out the right ideas from the good ideas. On this basis, you can create cross-functional teams united by a shared purpose and identify opportunites that may not seem immediately obvious but represent the potential places where the big battles will be won or lost. As you focus your precious resources on fewer things, you can move faster in the right direction and get ahead of all potential competition. Organizations implementing StoryDoing® make anything possible in a world where everything is not.

CHAPTER 15

Leading Change

"Most top management teams are not really teams at all because they won't sacrifice resources to help the team succeed. Only strong leaders can facilitate this level of cooperation."—Braden Kelley

C hange efforts don't happen by themselves; they must be led to completion. Change Leadership is one of the five keys to successful organizational change, and it can have a big impact on creating and sustaining the momentum of any change effort.

Many good leadership books are available to help you with advice on this topic. In this chapter we will highlight a few leadership frameworks from sources we believe do the best job of making change leadership understandable. We will focus specifically on the role of the change leader and the influence of leadership on your desired change outcomes.

The Role of a Leader in Change

If you look at The Five Keys to Successful Change™ in figure 15.1, you'll see that change leadership is one of those five keys.

Here are nine essential skills an effective change leadership team should possess:

1. position power
2. expertise
3. credibility
4. connectedness

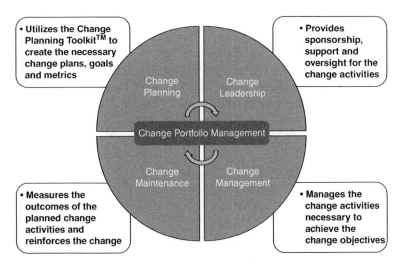

Figure 15.1   The Five Keys to Successful Change™

5. political savvy
6. influence
7. leadership ability
8. evangelism
9. accountability/ownership

And as we look at the entire scope and duration of any change effort (even a project), change leaders play a number of important roles in the planning, management, and maintenance of change. However, change leadership teams may lack some of the skills listed above if the following nine of The Eleven Change Roles™ are not represented on the team:

1. Authority Figures/Sponsors
2. Designers
3. Influencers
4. Integrators
5. Connectors
6. Resource Controllers/Investors
7. Troubleshooters
8. Evangelists/Storytellers
9. Endorsers/Supporters

You will notice some obvious overlap between the two lists, especially when you refer to the descriptions of The Eleven Change Roles™ in chapter 8.

Leading Change in the Face of Resistance

Change leaders must learn to recognize the many different ways people will try to defeat the change effort (or, at a minimum, to resist it). The change leadership team then must work together to craft thoughtful responses that take the sting out of the change and help to create buy-in instead. John P. Kotter and Lorne A. Whitehead in their book *Buy-in* did a great job highlighting how people often seek to kill change efforts utilizing tactics such as confusion, ridicule, delay, and fear-mongering supported by phrases like the following:[1]

- "It's too simplistic to work."
- "This is not the right time."
- "We tried it before, and it didn't work."

When change leadership teams are prepared for resistance such as this, their odds of guiding their change effort successfully to its desired outcomes increase considerably.

Leadership Must Control the Flow

In chapter 4 I introduced my Flow of Change Model v1.5 briefly (see figure 15.2), and the eleven different change states along with the Triple T Metric. This metric is designed to measure organizational agility by allowing change leaders to measure the time it takes the organizationto transform through each of the eleven change states in similar change efforts. We will now revisit the model in much greater detail because change leaders have a part to play during all eleven stages of the change process. Let's look at each in turn and at the role of change leaders in each.

1. Start with the Status Quo

For the change leadership team to be successful and for the change planning efforts to achieve their intended outcomes, the team spend time on achieving a comprehensive understanding of the status quo. There are many different questions you'll want to ask yourselves including the following:

- Why do people like things the way they are?
- What's painful about the current way of doing things?

Because of the importance of this stage, we devoted chapter 3 to it.

2. Identify the Problem

Good leaders consume a huge volume of data and human inputs and intuitively identify what matters. In this context, what matters is that you identify the problem accurately. Pick the wrong problem, and you'll plan, design, and implement the wrong set of behavior changes, changes that ultimately don't achieve the intended outcomes. You may want to refresh your memory on what we discussed in two earlier chapters:

- Chapter 3: "Understanding the Current State"
- Chapter 4: "Exploring Readiness for Change and Transitions"

The questions highlighted here and in the associated elements of the Change Planning Toolkit™ will help you better identify your problems.

3. Sell the Problem

One of the mistakes many leaders make (change leaders especially) is jumping to solutions too quickly. Before you begin creating solutions for the problem, you as change leader must first explain the identified problem and confirm that you've picked the right problem, defined it properly, and are explaining it in a way that makes sense. After understanding the problem correctly, you must then explain

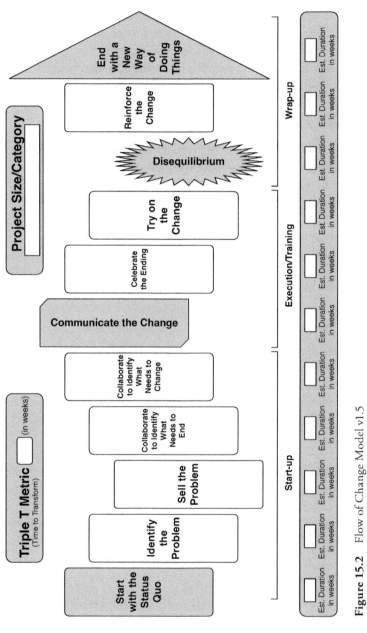

Figure 15.2 Flow of Change Model v1.5

why the problem is important and urgently needs solving so you can engage others throughout your organization in the change effort.

4. Collaborate to Identify What Needs to End

As you begin implementing solutions, you must first discuss with your change leadership team what behaviors need to end. For behavior change to occur, people must stop doing something and start doing something else. Thus, the first half of finding a solution is to determine what people need to stop doing and how to effectively convince them that they need to do so.

5. Collaborate to Identify What Needs to Change

In this stage (and the previous one), you as change leader may use the Stop/Start/Continue Worksheet as one of the tools to help you identify both what needs to end and what needs to change—that is, what people can start doing or continue doing but maybe in a somewhat different way.

6. Communicate the Change

While this stage is focused on communications, all of the work does not occur in this stage. All along the way change leaders should be determining key messages, targeting and segmentation, channels, channel availability, sequencing, and all of the other components that will contribute to successful communication of the change during this stage. Because it is during this stage when you open the curtains, so to speak, and let people know why the change is needed, what it is intended to achieve, how the change will unfold, and so on. Ultimately, you as change leader are responsible for clearly stating the expected outcomes of the change effort, delivering consistent messaging, modeling the behaviors required to support change, making the change personal, and reinforcing the behaviors that will lead to the desired change outcomes. Chapter 14 is devoted to this topic.

7. Celebrate the Ending

Too often we focus on the new components of the change and ignore the ones being replaced, whether these are behaviors, systems, or solutions. The peril in pursuing change in this manner is that it makes the change seem more optional. Smart change leaders recognize the service the old behaviors, systems, or solutions may have provided and emphasize that they are coming to an end. They hold a party or a funeral—whatever most clearly communicates that the old behaviors, systems, or solutions are no longer to be used in the future.

8. Try on the Change

Marketing uses the concept of ATR, an acronym that stands for awareness, trial, repeat to measure success in any campaign. Change leaders must utilize this simple framework, as the job of change leadership is to shepherd the change effort through all three stages. If you as change leader convince people only to participate in one or two ATR steps, your change effort will fail. In trying on the change it is wise to experiment and learn as you go. This process is also about building the trial phase in a way that helps you deal with the next stage: Disequilibrium.

9. Disequilibrium

Disequilibrium is the loss of balance in an ecosystem or market. When a new force or change is introduced into a system (such as an organization), disequilibrium occurs. Change is like dropping a sugar cube into a glass of water; the cube causes a splash and ripples on the surface of the water. This is disequilibrium. And if you wait long enough, the movement on the surface of the water will subside and below the surface the sugar cube will be absorbed into the water over time. It is important to note that if you add energy to the water in the form of heat, the absorption of the sugar cube will happen more quickly. The same is true for any kind of change. This period of disequilibrium when the status quo is disrupted and out of balance can be shortened by applying energy or effort to supporting people through the transition or transformation to the desired state and the new behaviors. This can be achieved using a variety of tools, including training, communications, and coaching.

10. Reinforce the Change

In much the same way we "Celebrate the Ending," we must also reinforce the change by making sure people have a chance to practice the new behaviors and work with the new system or solution. Reserve some of your communication channels in your communications strategy for celebrating individuals and their positive use of or reactions to the new behaviors, systems, or solutions. This will help reinforce that making the change is not optional. Consider having a small budget for rewarding the desired behavior changes. During this stage it is also useful to send communications with additional tips on how to get more out of the new behaviors, systems, or solutions. You can also provide refresher training via reference guides or how-to videos to reinforce the change as people continue to practice it.

11. End with a New Way of Doing Things

You should end with people practicing the new behaviors, systems, or solutions and begin to decommission the old systems or solutions that have been replaced (if you have not already executed a hard stop). You should continue to reinforce the change during this decommissioning period, and you should now also be able to make your final Triple T Metric measurements (Time to Transform, see "Measuring Organizational Agility" in chapter 4). This is also the time for any other final measurements of whether you achieved your desired change outcomes (including behavior changes).

Conclusion

I've chosen a wave to represent the different stages of a change effort because every change effort will have its ups and downs, and it is up to the change leaders to maintain the momentum pushing the change effort forward.

Quick Wins versus Momentum

The success of a change effort depends not on achieving quick wins, but on maintaining consistent, positive, forward momentum throughout all of the transitions. One of the ways to do this is to take an agile approach to change and to segment your overall change effort into a series of work packages that you can properly staff, execute, and celebrate. Many change efforts and projects get off to a roaring start, achieve a few quick wins, but stall when longer, more substantial pieces of the work must be completed, often with only limited communication and little visible progress. The change effort then begins to lose the support of key stakeholders (and potentially resources) as members of the change leadership team begin to lose enthusiasm, break solidarity, and withdraw support. This dooms the effort, preventing it from ever being completed as intended.

Momentum beats quick wins, and engaging in a more visual, collaborative, agile change planning method like the one described in this book will lead you to more successful change efforts because these methods can help you maintain momentum. The Agile Change Management Kanban is a useful tool that toolkit buyers can leverage to visualize and track change effort progress.

Summary

In this chapter we looked at the role of the change leaders and examined how leadership can influence your desired change outcomes. This included revisiting The Eleven Change Roles™ and The Five Keys to Successful Change™. In addition, we looked at nine essential skills an effective change leadership team should possess, and we discussed how to be successful leading change in the face of resistance.

We then looked at my Flow of Change Model v1.5 and investigated in great detail the contributions change leaders must make during each stage. Finally, we closed with a discussion of how maintaining consistent, positive forward momentum is more important than achieving some quick wins early on in the process.

Guest Expert

Tanveer Naseer, MSc. (@TanveerNaseer)

An award-winning and internationally acclaimed leadership writer, author of the book *Leadership Vertigo*, keynote speaker, and founder of Tanveer Naseer Leadership, a leadership coaching firm.

www.TanveerNaseer.com

How Successful Leaders Champion Change in Today's Organizations

Although change has become a standard feature of today's business environment, change leadership still remains elusive and difficult for many leaders to effectively promote and encourage within their organization.

One key reason for this is the fact that many leaders continue to operate from the vantage point of being reactive instead of *being responsive* to the inevitable changes that are a part of today's leadership. Add to this the increasing demands on our time, energy, and resources—and the increasing number of distractions in today's workplaces—and it becomes understandable why change leadership remains a major challenge for many leaders.

However, despite the fast pace of today's global business environment, we can be successful in leading change in our organization by employing the following steps:

1. Don't Just Tell, But Show Why These Change Initiatives Matter

When it comes to promoting any change initiative, it's often helpful to remember something we were told by our mothers: don't forget to eat your vegetables. Now for most of us, this was something that was often repeated to us because our parents wanted to make sure that we developed healthy eating habits. And yet, despite our parents' best efforts and after hearing about all the studies showing the importance of vegetables to our long-term health, many of us still struggle to get our daily servings of vegetables in our diet.

Why is that? Why is there such a struggle to eat more vegetables despite what we now know and what our mothers told us growing up? The reason is simple; although we might understand the health benefits, what was missing in all of these messages is something that's critical to our eating habits: we like to eat food that appeals to our taste buds.

What this reveals is a very important point about how to successfully lead change in your organization. Specifically, to promote any change initiative among your employees, you can't operate from the vantage point that you know what's best for your organization and that consequently your employees should simply fall in line with your plans.

Rather, what's required to be successful at change leadership is to ensure that your employees understand *why* this initiative matters in terms of their ability to be successful in achieving your organization's shared purpose.

We have to remember that it's only when we connect our change initiative to what matters to our employees that they'll get on board with making it a reality. Otherwise, just like the vegetables we had on our plates as kids, your change initiatives will simply end up being pushed aside in favor of focusing on the things that really matter to those you lead.

2. Don't Confuse Conviction with Inflexibility

One characteristic that's critical to successful change leadership is demonstrating an unwavering commitment and resolve to making this change work. However, the danger we need to be mindful of is not falling into the trap of becoming inflexible in how we address the needs and concerns of those we serve.

As much as our employees will be reassured by our sense of confidence and assuredness in the vision that's driving our change leadership, we also need to demonstrate a willingness to listen and understand what our employees have to say about it, especially as the process moves forward and unexpected issues or challenges surface.

To ensure the full commitment of our employees to this change, we have to show them that we're not walking into these conversations thinking we have all the answers. Instead, our employees need to see that we're interested in listening to what they have to say so we can identify course corrections we might need to make to ensure the employees' effectiveness in guiding this change forward.

Again, it is important that leaders show a strong conviction and belief in their change leadership. But it's equally important that our employees get the message that we're more interested in empowering them to become full participants in making this change our new reality.

3. Clarify Expectations for What This Initiative Will Look Like

When it comes to change leadership, the common focus tends to be on creating grand visions of what these initiatives will create, of the new opportunities for the organization they will open up, and on what key steps need to be taken to get this process started.

Unfortunately, it's at this point in the process where many leaders pull back on their active participation, thinking that once tasks are delegated, there's no need for elaboration or follow-up as things progress.

In order to understand the challenge this presents in terms of being successful in our change leadership, we have to recognize something that's a part of human nature. Specifically, all of us have natural apprehensions regarding change because of the inherent uncertainty accompanying change, uncertainty about what we'll experience going forward.

That's why when you're communicating your change initiative to your employees, you need to provide clarity as to what the change will look like in practice. You need to explain what your employees should expect from you as things progress and, in particular, how you'll respond to potential obstacles they might come across as the process continues.

Such efforts will help to encourage a sense of belonging, inclusion, and shared ownership among your employees because the clarity you provide will remind them that their contributions are directly tied to transforming this idea into reality.

The undeniable truth about today's leadership is that the increasing demands and distractions we face will not lessen over time, but will continue to grow for many years to come. That's why it's critical that we ensure the initiatives we guide through our change leadership help move us closer to achieving our shared purpose.

CHAPTER 16

Innovation Is All about Change

"Innovation is anything but business as usual."—Anonymous

I nnovation is all about change. Innovation comes from identifying and capitalizing on changes in customer behavior, technology, society, regulations, and so on. But innovation is not just about external changes. Any true innovation also inflicts change on employees, partners, and customers in order to create competitive advantage. The increasing pace of innovation contributes to the accelerating need for change in our organizations and requires them to become more agile and flexible. At the same time, the new market realities of shorter life cycles for products and services require organizations to focus on continually evolving customer needs and requirements. This in itself represents a change for many organizations. We'll investigate each of the above intersections between innovation and change in turn.

Tracking a Moving Target

Successful innovation requires making meaningful connections and sustaining productive dialogue with your existing and prospective customers. But it also requires building meaningful conversations and connections with employees, suppliers, and a host of other members of your organization's ecosystem (which includes the aforementioned employees, suppliers, and other groups). We will investigate the role of stakeholder groups other than customers and their influence on innovation and change later in this chapter.

For now let's focus on how you as change leader must connect with your customers, uncover that key insight, and understand where the unmet needs lie and how best to meet them in order to create successful innovations.

One thing to keep in mind is that innovation and invention are not the same things. Inventions are interesting and potentially useful, but innovations must be valuable enough to cause people to replace their existing solution (even the do-nothing solution) with the new solution.

One way to track the moving targets of customer insights and technology capabilities is to build a global sensing network (see figure 16.1). Building such a network allows you to fight the innovation war outside your organization—not inside.

The old way of succeeding in business was to hire the most clever, experienced, and motivated people you could afford and then direct them to come up with the best customer solutions possible. Then these employees organized and executed their production and marketing plans predictably and efficiently, and did their best

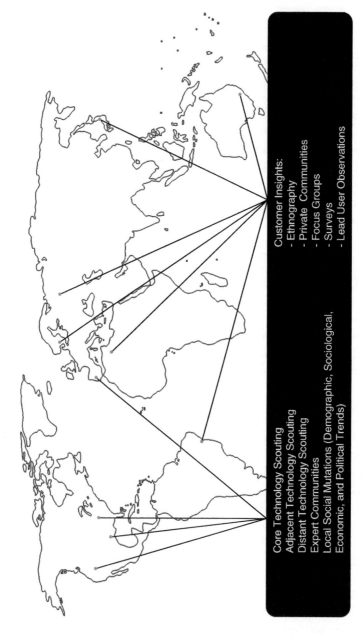

Customer Insights:
- Ethnography
- Private Communities
- Focus Groups
- Surveys
- Lead User Observations

Core Technology Scouting
Adjacent Technology Scouting
Distant Technology Scouting
Expert Communities
Local Social Mutations (Demographic, Sociological,
Economic, and Political Trends)

Figure 16.1 Building a Global Sensing Network

to outmaneuver the competition. But the battlefield of business success is changing. Future business success will be built upon the ability to:

1. utilize expert communities;
2. identify and gather technology trend information, customer insights, and local social mutations from around the globe;
3. mobilize the organization to utilize resources and information that are often beyond its control;
4. still organize and execute production and marketing plans predictably and efficiently amidst all this complexity.

At the same time, market leadership will be increasingly determined not by the ability to outmaneuver the competition in a known market, but by the ability to identify and solve the key unknowns in markets that will continue to become more global and less defined. Future market leaders will be organizations that build superior global sensing networks and do a better job at understanding the inputs from these networks to select the optimal actionable insights for innovation.

You should now be asking yourself two questions:

1. What does a global sensing network look like?
2. How do I build one?

The purpose of a global sensing network is to allow an organization to collect and connect the partial insights and ideas that will form the basis of the organization's next generation of customer solutions. This involves collecting and connecting:

1. customer insights
   - ethnography
   - private communities
   - focus groups
   - surveys
   - lead user observation
2. core technology trends
3. adjacent technology trends
4. distant technology trends
5. local social mutations
   - demographic trends
   - sociological trends
   - economic trends
   - political trends (including regulation)
   - behavioral trends

6. expert communities
   - university research
   - government research
   - corporate research
   - charitable research
   - hobbyists

Building a global sensing network requires you to start from the inside out. You have to take a look around inside your organization and see what employees you have, what natural connections they have, and where they are currently located on the globe. At the same time, you need to understand how employees in your organization naturally connect with each other, and you must define what core, adjacent, and distant technologies mean in the context of your organization. You must also find out what tools you have inside the organization for managing insights, expertise, and information within the organization and what expert communities you may already have connections to.

Begin by establishing your global sensing network inside your organization first before building it out the rest of the way with the resources and connections you will naturally need outside your organization. Starting on the inside will allow you to get some really great feedback from employees on the connections you will need to foster and manage outside of your organization. This approach will also enable you to prepare the information sharing and internal communications systems you need to improve innovation inputs and outputs.

Many organizations likely are already gathering some level of customer insight information from ethnography, private communities, focus groups, surveys, lead user observation, and so on. But often these organizations do not have a good infrastructure, policies, or procedures for sharing this information. To create increased innovation capability and achieve innovation excellence, you should conduct system experiments that make customer information more available throughout different levels of your organization.

Next, you should leverage your employees and existing partnerships to reach outside the organization to establish stronger communication channels with the relevant expert communities, including those focused on university research, government research, charitable research, corporate research (industry associations and competitors), and you should also connect to inventors or hobbyists.

Based on the connections you've built by this point, you should have identified where you have good people internally to provide information on local social mutations, customer insights, tech trends, and various types of research. And you can see where you have gaps in your global sensing network; you need to fill these using formal or informal connections to experts outside the company.

One of the main reasons for building a global sensing network is that innovation can come from anywhere, and so you need to be listening everywhere. You must be listening so you can amplify, combine, and triangulate the weak signals you might pick up and find the next innovation your organization is capable of delivering—before the competition does. After all, there is a war for innovation out there, and the only unknown is who's going to win. Can you sense changes in customer wants and needs fast enough? Can your organization adapt quickly enough to provide the desired products and services in a profitable and timely manner?

Taking a More Flexible Approach to Innovation

To achieve sustainable success at innovation, you must embed a repeatable process and way of thinking in your organization, and therefore it is important to have a simple common language and guiding framework of infinite innovation that all employees can easily grasp. If innovation becomes too complex or seems too difficult, then people will stop pursuing or supporting it.

Some organizations try to achieve this simplicity and make innovation seem more achievable by viewing it as a project-driven activity. But a project approach to innovation will prevent it from ever becoming a way of life in your organization. Instead, you must position innovation as something infinite, a pillar of the organization, something with its own quest for excellence—a professional practice to be committed to.

Combining the best practices of innovation excellence with a few new ingredients results in a simple framework organizations can use to guide a sustainable pursuit of innovation: the Eight I's of Infinite Innovation™ (see figure 16.2). This framework anchors a collaborative innovation process. Here is the framework and some of the many points organizations must consider during each stage of the process:

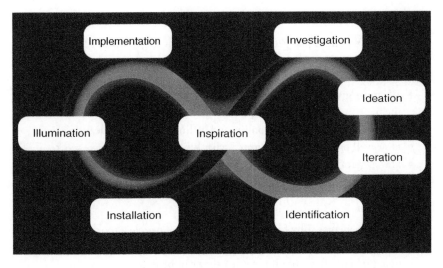

Figure 16.2   Eight I's of Infinite Innovation™

1. Inspiration

- Employees are constantly navigating an ever-changing world both in their home context and as they travel the world for business or pleasure or even across various pages in the web browser of their PC, tablet, or smartphone.
- What do employees see as they move through the world that inspires them and possibly the innovation efforts of their company?
- What do they see technology making possible soon that wasn't possible before?
- The first time going through the questions we are looking for inspiration regarding what to do, and the second time through we are looking to be inspired regarding how to do it.
- What inspiration do we find in the ideas that are selected for implementation, illumination, and/or installation?

2. Investigation

- What can we learn from the various pieces of inspiration that employees come across?
- How do the isolated elements of inspiration collect and connect? Or do they?
- What customer insights are hidden in these pieces of inspiration?
- What jobs to be done are most underserved and are worth digging deeper on?
- Which unmet customer needs we see are worth addressing?
- Which are the most promising opportunities and which might be the most profitable ones?

3. Ideation

- We don't want to just get lots of ideas; we want to get lots of good ideas.
- Insights and inspiration from the first two stages increase relevance and depth of the ideas.
- We must give people a way of sharing their ideas in a way that feels safe for them.
- How can we best integrate online and offline methods of ideation?
- How well have we communicated what kinds of innovation we seek?
- Have we trained our employees in a variety of creativity methods?

4. Iteration

- No idea emerges fully formed, so we must give people a tool that allows them to contribute ideas in a way that others can build on and help uncover the potential fatal flaws of ideas so that they can be overcome.

- We must prototype ideas and conduct experiments to validate assumptions and test potential stumbling blocks or unknowns so we can learn how to make the idea and its prototype stronger.
- Are we instrumenting for learning as we conduct each experiment?

5. Identification

- In what ways do we make it difficult for customers to unlock the inherent value of this potentially innovative solution?
- What are the biggest potential barriers to adoption of the solution?
- What changes do we need to make from a finance, marketing, design, or sales perspective to make it easier for customers to access the value of this new solution?
- Which ideas are we best positioned to develop and bring to market?
- What resources do we lack to realize the promise of each idea?
- Based on all of the experiments, data, and markets, which ideas should we select?

You'll see in the framework that our thinking loops back through inspiration again before proceeding to implementation. There are two main reasons for this. First, if employees aren't inspired by the ideas you have selected to commercialize and the potential implementation issues you have identified, then you either have selected the wrong ideas or you've got the wrong employees. Second, at this intersection you might want to go back through the first five stages from the perspective of implementation before actually starting to implement your ideas, *or* you may widen your quest for inspiration and input to a wider internal audience for inclusion before entering the implementation stage.

6. Implementation

- What are the most effective and efficient ways to make, market, and sell this new solution?
- How long will it take us to develop the solution?
- Do we have access to the resources we will need to produce the solution?
- Are we strong in the channels of distribution that are most suitable for delivering this solution?

7. Illumination

- Is the need for the solution obvious to potential customers?
- Are we launching a new solution as part of an existing product or service category or are we creating a new category?

- Does this new solution fit into our existing brand and does it represent something potential customers will trust us to sell to them?
- How much value translation do we need to do for potential customers to help them understand how this new solution fits into their lives and why it is a must-have?
- Do we need to just explain this potential innovation to customers because it anchors to something that they already understand, or do we need to educate them on the value it will add to their lives?

8. Installation

- How do we best make this new solution an accepted part of everyday life for a large number of people?
- How do we remove access barriers and make it as easy as possible for people to adopt this new solution and even tell their friends about it?
- How do we provide for learning during the installation process to include new learnings about customers in the process for potential updates to the solution?

The Eight I's of Infinite Innovation™ framework is designed to be a continuous learning process, a process without end as the outputs of one round become inputs for the next round. The framework is also ideally suited to power a wave of new organizational transformations that are coming as an increasing number of organizations (including Hallmark) begin to move from a product-centered organizational structure to one centered on customer needs. The power of this new approach is that it focuses the organization on delivering the solutions customers need even as those needs continue to change. This is very different from focusing only on how to make a particular product (or set of products) better.

As you move away from the project approach to innovation, consider using the Eight I's of Infinite Innovation™ to influence your organization's mind-set and to anchor your common language of innovation. The framework is great for guiding conversations and making your innovation outputs stronger; it will contribute to your quest for innovation excellence.

Managing Change is the Key to Successful Infinite Innovation

Companies that successfully innovate continuously have one thing in common: they are good at managing change. Change comes from many sources, but where innovation is concerned, the main sources of change are incremental innovation and disruptive innovation.

The small changes comprising incremental innovations often represent evolutions of existing products and services, and the organization, customers, and other stakeholders can usually adjust and accept them with fairly logical explanations.

Figure 16.3 Managing Innovation is about Managing Change

However, the large changes generated by disruptive innovations often come from the connected imagination of the organization, and these forward leaps for the business often disrupt not only the market but the internal workings of the organization as well. Disruptive innovations also tend to require not just explanation but an extended period of education for the stakeholders affected.

The change injected into organizations by innovation ebbs and flows across the whole organization's ecosystem (as shown in figure 16.3).

Let's explore the categories of change displayed in figure 16.3 using Apple's iPod as an example:

1. **Customer Changes**
   a. Any disruptive innovation requires a company to imagine for the customers something they find difficult to imagine for themselves. Go too far past customers' ability to imagine how the new product or service represents a solution to a real problem in their lives, and customer adoption of the innovation will be far below expectations.
   b. For the Apple iPod to be successful, customers needed to see Apple as a company to trust for reliable consumer electronics, not just computer hardware. Customers also needed to be able to imagine what it might mean to download and use music digitally (without physical media).

2. **Employee Changes**
   a. Disruptive innovations typically require employees to do things in a new way and that can be uncomfortable even if employees only have to imagine the same things as customers.

    b. But in this case, employees had to acquire lots of new knowledge and skills. Apple support employees had to learn to support a different, less technically savvy customer. Other employees had to learn how to build effective partnerships with the music industry.

3. **Supplier Changes**

    a. Innovations that disrupt the status quo can require suppliers to work with an organization in new ways. Some disruptive innovations may require drastic supplier changes akin to those suppliers had to make to support just-in-time (JIT) manufacturing.

    b. For Apple, this meant working with suppliers to source components at the higher volumes and shorter lead times required for success in consumer electronics. This also meant finding some new suppliers who could handle the different market requirements and volumes.

4. **Distribution Changes**

    a. Often larger innovations disrupt whole distribution channels and this can cause challenges for incumbent organizations (i.e., Dell Direct versus Compaq and big box retailers).

    b. Going into consumer electronics led Apple to build relationships with big box stores like Target, Walmart, and Costco. Apple also had to build a completely new digital distribution system for music (iTunes).

5. **Marketing Changes**

    a. New products and services (especially disruptive ones) can require marketing to find and build relationships with different types of customers, to speak to customers in new and different ways, and to potentially reach them through different channels.

    b. Marketing had to begin shifting the Apple brand from computing to lifestyle. This included changing the company name from Apple Computer to Apple in 2007. Marketing also had to learn how to connect with mass market consumers and to help them imagine how this new hardware/software combination would enhance their lifestyle. All of this was no small task.

6. **Operations Changes**

    a. In addition to supply chain changes, the organization may need to adapt to disruptive innovations by hiring different types of employees, retraining current employees, accounting for revenue in a different way, or doing production in a new way.

    b. The Apple iPod was an experience sell, and this shone a spotlight on the fact that Apple didn't have a place where customers could see as well as experience the products. This led to the creation of Apple retail stores. Meanwhile, Apple's finance and operations groups had to adapt to the change from low-volume, high-price items to high-volume, low-price items. Apple also had to build out a resource-intensive e-commerce operation that didn't exist before (lots of technology and infrastructure investment).

Notice that figure 16.3 has arrows going in a circular direction. This is because there is a cyclical relationship. In the beginning of the innovation process the satellites influence what the innovation will look like (new suppliers, new production capabilities, ideas from partners/suppliers, new marketing methods, component innovations, etc.). But as the innovation goes into full commercialization, the change direction takes on an outward focus.

It should now be clear that as organizations imagine how to take creative ideas and transform them into valuable innovations in the marketplace, they should also envision all required changes and plan for their execution. This is no small feat. But with proper planning, organizational learning, and agility, any organization can improve its ability to execute and even anticipate the changes necessary to implement its next disruptive innovation.

Summary

In this chapter we investigated three different ways that innovation is (or should be) all about change and how to cope with this fact. We looked at how innovation comes from identifying and capitalizing on changes in customer behavior, technology, society, and regulations, among other things. We also looked at a framework that enables you to take a more flexible, more agile, iterative approach to innovation that has inspiration at its core. Finally, we looked at how any true innovation also inflicts change on employees, partners, and customers in order to successfully create a competitive advantage.

It should be clear that the increasing pace of innovation contributes to an accelerating need for change in our organizations and requires them to become more agile and flexible.. Is your organization ready to cope with accelerating change and innovation?

Guest Expert—Case Study

Babak Forutanpour (@babakf)

A Curious Soul. Engineer. UX Technologist. VFX Artist. Founder of Qualcomm's FLUX and cocreator of Don't Dream Alone. Creator of the @TheAryaBall.

www.DontDreamAlone.com

Don't Dream Alone: Story of Grass-Roots Innovation in a Fortune 500 Company

The Thrill of "404 – Page Not Found"

"That is brilliant Brian," I exclaimed. "I would never have thought of that!" When I asked the team how we could help improve Qualcomm's imaging solution, I wasn't expecting Brian would come up with such a clever way to enhance its auto white balance algorithm (AWB). AWB is the process of removing any colors cast by the light source. This allows snapshots to have more lifelike colors. He continued, "We can take better pictures by turning on the microphones. We are not just building a point-and-shoot camera. The camera is part of a smartphone, which has lots of other sensors. If we turn on the microphone and try to listen for buzzing of fluorescent lights, we can tell if the user is in sunlight or artificial light."

We sat silently staring at one another, with perplexed looks on our faces. None of us had ever thought that you could use sound to take a better picture. This discovery would be the first of many 404s that we would have together!

"404" is clubspeak for discovering a novel solution to an existing problem or a solution to a problem that others do not even know exist. It occurs when you do a Google search on your idea, and the results come back as "404 – Error. Page Not Found." After hitting our first 404 together, we knew that we were hooked. We would be forever chasing that initial high, craving another hit of dopamine or whatever it is that is released in the system when the brain makes a pattern nobody else in the world has ever seen.

A few seconds later, Brian went on to share that he could also use the speakers on the phone to take better pictures. "By sending an ultrasonic pulse, the phone can listen for reflections. If it hears any echoes, then there is a good chance the user is indoors." A round of high-fives went around the room!

Brian's idea inspired me to think about how to use the other sensors on the phone to take a better picture. I was suddenly struck by how we could leverage the device's global positioning system (GPS) and clock. "Hey, if the camera knows it is 9 p.m., and it is being used in San Diego, then it can narrow down the light source to artificial ones since it knows the sun has set!" Another round of high-fives.

After the meeting, I literally ran to speak to Bob, the head our camera team's 3A systems (AWB, autofocus, auto-exposure). He and his colleague were dumbfounded by the fact that they had not thought about using other sensors on the device to take better pictures after all these years.

Bob helped us fill in the gaps in our knowledge and encouraged us to build a simple proof of concept. We tested our hunch; it worked, and together we filed our very first Invention Disclosure Form (IDF) with the Patent Review Board (PRB) at Qualcomm. We crossed our fingers that the team of subject matter experts liked our invention and would set aside a budget to patent our idea. Plaque US 12/835,454 hangs on my wall to this day—a reminder of how that little experiment turned out.

What happened over the course of the next six years amazes me to this day. Who could have imagined that the eight of us would go on to inspire thousands of others in the company across four continents to take a pause every two weeks, even if only for ninety minutes, to work cross-departmentally to peer into the future together, each person with his or her own unique lens. We didn't know that our work would lead us to the office of our CEO, inspire numerous R&D projects, and capture 70 patents in 70 months. And we did all of this during our lunch breaks.

One Light Bulb At A Time

The stories and best practices we share here are not intended for innovation consultants or chief innovation officers only. Our motivation is to speak to employees directly, and we hope that if you want to work in an environment that celebrates creative thinking as well as executing corporate initiatives, you have the power to be the change.

Being innovative in a large company is generally not valued as much as leaders often say it is. The fact is that mature companies must run as fast as they can to stay ahead of the competition since their customers not only know what they want but have already told other potential suppliers. Companies generally do not have much patience for exploring revolutionary ideas. Middle management measures how many lines of code are written and how much faster a widget is made. If you want to have greater balance in your work and want to blend technical thinking with applied imagination, you must bring that change about yourself. We share with you the story of how starting with yourself and helping light a light bulb in the minds of others one at a time, soon the whole company while shine brighter.

Team Looking Glass

Who was in the room that day in mid-2009? The founders of what would become Qualcomm's employee-run innovation program, Forward Looking User Experience (FLUX). How did we know each other? Most of us didn't. I barely knew some of them myself when I asked them to attend my meeting. All we really had at that first meeting was a team name we picked: Team Looking Glass.

You see, I started FLUX out of frustration. I was fed up working in a department where outside ideas were not encouraged and where we were told, "It's better to polish a turd on your own project than to be innovative outside these walls." Not finding the space I needed to be creative, I decided to create my own. I chose to start a little experiment. I was curious to see what would happen if I asked eight employees from different departments to join me for lunch every two weeks to see if together we could be innovative. All I asked was that there be no use of electronic devices and for them to give the program an honest shot for six consecutive meetings.

Together, we had good representation of talent from various departments in the company: imaging, audio, graphics, power, display, and business development. We were all in our twenties and thirties, six men and two women.

In the first meeting I explained our goal. It was to be first—first with a solution to a known problem or first to think of a problem others didn't even know existed. To me, this was a bigger challenge than finding the next billion-dollar idea. Qualcomm had enough money to explore tens of big ideas, and one would eventually hit. It didn't take a genius to realize that putting our chips into anything that ran off a battery, like cars or robots, had the potential to be the next S-curve we jump to. I didn't want us to concern ourselves with some needle or the notion of moving it. I wanted us to come up with ideas that would delight, something that would evoke an emotion of surprise when shared with others. We wanted ideas that would literally tickle our brain as a new connection is made. While most ideas are a dime a dozen, by definition, novel ones are not.

"While I want us to have fun, this is not a team building exercise. Happy hour does not start until 6 p.m.," I explained. "I would like for us to measure our performance by the number of 404s we hit. I will be taking meeting minutes to keep inventorship clear because patents may be filed. Patents are a way for the company to reserve 20 years' time to decide if they want to do deeper dives on our ideas. There may be a bit of homework involved as I will email you pain points that your colleagues have submitted, which I ask you to ponder before our meetings."

If One Team Is Good, Are Two Better?

After several months of having these fascinating discussions and five of our best ideas already approved by the PRB for patent filing, I knew that I wanted more. Once every two weeks just wasn't enough action. I started to think about starting a second team.

Would lighting strike twice? I decided to find out. I sat down one day and went through our corporate online phone directory. Scrolling through pictures of employees from different social and technical backgrounds, I sent emails to 20 people who caught my eye. I knew 20 was a good number because 6 would most likely be no-shows and another 6 would drop out over time, leaving me with 8. Jeff Bezos of Amazon is quoted as saying that a team you can feed with two pizzas is all you need for most projects of reasonable scale.

Knowing that free food for the first meeting always helps draw a crowd, I asked our department secretary to order a couple of pies. The turnout was pretty much as expected, and I shared with my soon-to-be friends the journey I wanted us to take together. While some were skeptical and soon dropped out after just a few meetings, the success of the first FLUX team motivated others to stick around to see if together we could stump a Google search too.

There were some real rock stars on that team, and after a few meetings, it happened! Our first 404 emerged when the team collaborated on how to minimize loud noises during a call. How cool would it be if during a phone call you could point your phone in the direction of an annoying sound, and after you bring the phone back to your ear, the person on the other end of the call no longer hears that noise? This was possible by combining orientation sensors with the active noise cancelation algorithm to attenuate or amplify sounds using beam forming techniques. When we shared this idea with our audio team, the team members loved it and provided us with an expert to provide missing details for a crude prototype and patent application.

Several months later, another light bulb went on in the minds of the team called Team Rabbit Hole. We realized the problem with camera phones wasn't the image quality that team Looking Glass had helped improve, but was with the user experience. The team found a novel way to help find the picture or video a user would want to share from among a vast number of thumbnails. We outlined a system using paper mockups that showed how pressing on the LCD screen during the moments when one is recording particularly interesting video would make it easier to sort the media later. This way, users could sort media based on "good moment points" rather than by date or file size. In fact, the harder users pressed on the LCD, the more they were marking those moments as particularly interesting. The multimedia PRB loved the claim set, as did the imaging product manager who felt it was a strong differentiator.

Because I was still not content brainstorming with two teams every two weeks, I launched a third team. Members of that team not only reached 404 multiple times as well, but some of my closest friends were on that team. The team also had the coolest name: members called it "What The Flux!"

The Real Aha Moment

What happened next took me by total surprise.

As it turns out, Anthony liked being on Team Looking Glass very much and saw how I was able to repeat that magic two more times with teams Rabbit Hole and WTFlux!, so he wanted to start his own team.

Soon, Anthony started team Dreamweavers, and his team was also good at turning on light bulbs. One idea I recall was a clever way to help those who could not afford large data plans in third world countries to participate in social media sites like Facebook. The system allowed people to mark pictures they wanted to share with their friends and then upload just one. If enough people "liked" that picture, Facebook would then connect to the phone and pull a few more of the tagged pictures, collecting a small micropayment from those who wanted to see the pictures. This payment would be credited to the content creator to help offset his or her data plan costs. This wasn't just great for sharing selfies or pictures of special events like a wedding, but could also help create income for those who reported weather or other news events to nearby towns.

As word started to spread around the Qualcomm campus about these mini innovation teams over in Building AV, I no longer had to go through the phone directory to pull in members but was starting to get emails from folks who wanted to join. I had to create a waiting list to keep up with the demand. Fortunately, Jose stepped up to start a fifth team. Soon afterward, Mary started the sixth team and Maritza the seventh. Eventually, there were FLUX teams all around the campus. It was so rewarding to see those who wanted to daydream with me turn into dream catchers as well.

The 10th Floor

One day while walking on campus, I noticed a poster that presented our CEO as keynote speaker for a Women in Engineering event. I decided to reach out to him to see if he would also be interested in meeting with our club members and helping us celebrate our upcoming third anniversary. Minutes after sending that email, I received his response: "Happy to do so."

We met with Dr. Paul Jacobs, and he was so pleased to hear what we had accomplished with little or no resources outside of the patent review process that was available to all employees. He gave us a pat on the back and asked how he could help.

During FLUX's third anniversary, Paul Jacobs stood on stage and thanked us for working across departmental lines to drive Qualcomm's technology forward. It was especially rewarding that he stayed for the entire 90 minutes given his extremely busy schedule. I was happy to see that he participated in the portion of the program where we asked attendees to form groups of five to experience how much fun it can be to brainstorm, even on such common everyday items as a coffee mug, highlighter pen, or light bulb. The event was a huge success and helped the club reach more employees.

Big in Japan

With Paul shining a bright light on us, FLUX began to grow internationally. Soon I was getting requests from Qualcomm employees in Brazil, the United Kingdom, Canada, Singapore, Shanghai, India, Australia, and Japan who wanted to start their own mini innovation teams. I put together a training program through which employees who had joined a mailing list created for their territory could then pick a lead to be trained by me via Skype. It was amazing to witness the creative energy of the teams outside headquarters. I sensed that some of these satellite offices had something to prove, that they are not just great at execution, but should be given more funding for R&D as well. The team from Hyderabad, India, was particularly capable of seeing applications of technology two or three moves ahead of others. Some of their ideas around head-mounted displays were outstanding in their novelty and usefulness (e.g., US 13/757,175).

Having a Voice

Prior to meeting with Paul, I had registered FLUX as a QClub, similar to those who ran the hockey or poker club, and this covered $500 a year in expenses. When we earned the support of our CEO, human resources offered assistance to us as it was needed. While we could have asked for considerably more, the team leads and I opted to simply ask for a larger pizza and beer budget. We knew that more money wouldn't help us but might make us complacent. Ideation doesn't have to be an expensive and formal process; you only need passionately curious employees, and we had plenty of those.

The other requirement in order for FLUX members to make a meaningful impact was for the company to give us a platform so we could be heard. The ability to share our ideas with a panel of experts who would guide us on next steps and at a minimum protect the discoveries with a patent was paramount. Fortunately, we worked at a company that was truly committed to listening to everyone's bright or dull ideas without prejudice.

Protecting Your Brand

With all the growth we were experiencing, there was one thing my fellow moderators and I insisted upon: protecting our brand. If we wanted to attract the star players and continue to get high-level meetings with R&D leaders and product managers, we needed to keep the FLUX brand associated with quality ideas.

That is why before any team would file an IDF, we asked their moderator to share the ideas with all other moderators first. Together, we would decide whether or not the idea was representative of the kind of work that we could brand with our label. While we never discouraged anyone from filing an IDF, we did ask some to use their own department charge code if we felt the idea was not novel enough.

Beyond Brainstorming: Culture of Curiosity and Transparency

The phrase, "I'm not good at this," was one of the things I started to hear as more and more people were dropping out of our meetings. I catered to those who were uncomfortable with the fuzzy front end of innovation by creating two new programs.

FLUXSparks involved booking a conference room, ordering pizza, and having members share a trip report with others. By offering a new avenue for sharing knowledge, we encouraged greater transparency in the company, and this potentially inspired new ways of thinking. I started the inaugural meeting with a report I had put together from my recent trip to the Consumer Electronics Show (CES). Soon, folks signed up to share their trip reports too. It was engaging to hear research reported at conferences and universities that many in the room had not been exposed to previously. FLUXSparks sessions became so popular that short of booking our auditorium, there wasn't a room big enough to hold everyone. To meet the pressing demand, we started to stream our events live for those who were turned away at the door or worked in remote offices.

The other program we created was FLUXScreenings. Here, the club's goal was getting folks together during lunch every month or so in order to watch and discuss all the fascinating videos that were going around on the web. The group was a hit from the start! I was soon getting emails with links to videos from folks who wanted me to share them at the next meeting. These videos covered everything from how geckos walk up walls to how the parachute for the Mars Rover was tested. These sessions did not have a single presenter, and so we were able to meet demand by booking two or three rooms and screening the curated list of videos in each room simultaneously.

What folks didn't realize was that both of these events were actually red herrings. While half the intention was to promote a culture of curiosity, our program's real goal was to get employees to mix. Our idea was that by increasing the level of transparency, the process would be more efficient and innovative. Getting folks to introduce themselves, describing what they are working on, and sharing pain points almost always leads to interesting follow-up discussions in the halls. There was one session where we spent 40 minutes just on introductions, which left us with only 20 minutes for the videos, and no one minded.

Club leaders also realized that some members did not want to spend 90 minutes consecutively on ideation and preferred to do it on their own time. That is why we created numerous mailing lists, called FLUXThreads, that allowed members to brainstorm with those outside their technical network asynchronously. We capped each list at 50 people in order to prevent threads from getting unwieldy. This simple method worked out well and led to one of my favorite ideas from the program. That was an idea based on putting a Bluetooth transmitter and receiver inside an AA battery. Having a connected battery in an electronic device not only allowed users to find their items—for example, their TV remote control—but allowed a parent to turn on or off devices—for example, their kid's GameBoy at dinner time. The battery could also notify others what its host device was doing, for example, telling a son that the smoke detector in his mother's house had gone off.

FLUXSparks, FLUXScreenings, and FLUXThreads helped the club grow to over 3,000 members, about 10 percent of the company.

Hired Guns

While helping manage the FLUX programs and committing to my day job, I was inspired to start another FLUX program, FLUXFocus. It started when one day a senior executive called me to ask me if I could pull together the most creative and technical people in FLUX and help him with an important project. After a few private sessions with the executive, I decided to formalize the process and allow product managers and others in the company to leverage our resources. FLUXFocus was a hit from the start. It was a win-win. Managers were able to get a fresh look at their problem, and employees felt good that they were able to learn about and potentially help another division excel.

I'm Good

As FLUX began to grow, I was eventually offered a position to run FLUX full time under the broader official innovation program called impaQt. I knew that the people I would be reporting to would have allowed me to run the club the way my moderators and I wanted, but FLUX was never an exit strategy for me. I loved working on 2D and 3D graphics as software engineer. As long as someone was going to pay me to work on movies or develop cool features for phones, I was happy. FLUX was a way for my friends and me to spend some time thinking about the future, not a replacement for our chosen craft.

I like being in the boat with my comrades, rowing with a paddle, and I never felt I would be fulfilled at the helm with just a bullhorn. Having the desire to be both creative and technical, harnessing my whole brain, meant that I wouldn't truly be happy doing just one of the two. Doing interesting research full time and running FLUX on the side was the perfect balance.

What Motivates Us

In his book, *Drive*, Daniel Pink discusses employee motivations. The main motivations are purpose, mastery, and autonomy. If your team members believe in the mission, the work is something they enjoy doing and want to get better at; when management then gets out of their way, that's when magic happens.

I didn't realize that at the time, but the reason FLUX resonated with so many in the company was for these very same reasons. We had our purpose when the patent review board began recognizing our discoveries and over time invested over $4 million to protect them.

We wanted to be the best anthropologists we could be. From the beginning, we saw hitting 404s as a sport, something we wanted to get better at. We met every two weeks to exercise our brain, teaching it how to be more observant and empathetic, which is the foundation for good ideas.

Finally, FLUX was successful because no one ever told us how to do our job. FLUX was our playground to do and think as we wished, and we kept our bosses out of the meetings. Every topic was fair game. We didn't shoot down one another's ideas too early in the brainstorming process.

Even though our meetings had an agenda of pain points based on what members had submitted a few days before, we always began by asking if anyone had topics to share or discuss first. We wanted folks to know that this was their club, and no one was going to tell them how to ideate. I recall one time a member wanted to talk about how it upset him when people wouldn't wait for him to come out of an elevator before getting in. While some would say that topic is better suited for the Otis Elevator Company than Qualcomm, we never wanted to shut anyone down. We openly discussed all pain points, while gently bending them toward something that was more in Qualcomm's domain. We eventually took that elevator seed of discussion and bent it all the way to the United States Patent and Trademark Office (USPTO).

Conclusion: The Power of 2 Percent

When I asked eight employees to have lunch with me as I needed a few friends to brainstorm in a very execution-focused company, I didn't know that one day thousands would be working shoulder to shoulder, across four continents, helping our company focus more intentionally on discovering latent customer needs. Numerous researched or commercialized features have their roots in our early work, and 70 of those systems benefit from an early publication date with a registered patent body. Our brainstorming club spawned four other programs helping engineer serendipity in the organization and strengthening a culture of curiosity and transparency that has immeasurable results.

Beyond a camera that uses the microphone to take better pictures and other breakthrough ideas, most in the club would agree that the biggest value of FLUX was the many relationships it helped create. Whether it was decorating the lobby windows of our headquarters with a thousand Post-it notes, which were used to spell "FLUX" in Christmas and Hanukkah colors, or having beers with the CEO at the local watering hole, the journey truly was the reward.

Why tell our story? Because I think our message is an important one: The power of 2 percent time. While many employees do not have the luxury to dedicate 20 percent of their time to research areas they choose, we are proof that 2 percent of time done cross-departmentally in a structured way can lead to substantial innovations. If you get employees to schedule 90 minutes every two weeks in Outlook, your company will make huge strides toward becoming more empathetic and nimble in meeting customer's needs.

By embracing our diversity and trusting each other enough to look foolish in front of one another as we brainstormed, we succeeded in pulling up a chair for anyone else who wanted a seat at the innovation roundtable. We showed that you can be innovative during your lunch breaks on a budget of $500/year, as long as you have passionately curious employees who don't want to dream alone.

CHAPTER 17

Project and Portfolio Management Are about Change

"Put simply, if you're not managing change, you're not managing the project."
—Kieran Wright, PMO Manager and PMP, Hewlett-Packard Enterprise

Projects change things. Project management is a disciplined approach to managing those changes (whether large or small). And portfolio management manages and balances a group of change efforts (that we choose to call projects instead of change programs). But projects, like change programs, are slow to start and quick to fail. We will look at how our visual toolkit can help project and portfolio managers get their projects off to a better start and help make their project portfolio more comprehensive.

1. Every project is a change effort. Every project changes something.
2. Portfolio management is therefore the practice of managing a portfolio of change efforts.
3. Project management therefore is actually a subdiscipline of change management, utilized to bring order to the chaos of managing a change effort to its successful conclusion.
4. Project planning is therefore a subdiscipline of change planning, utilized to plan how the tasks should be ordered and readied for a project manager to manage.

When all of these components are taken together I hope it is clear that successful change management pulls together the talents of a whole host of people including:

- a skilled project manager to manage risks, issues, scope, schedule, budget, and resources;
- an insightful communications manager who thinks like a marketer, carefully identifying the distinct segments you will be communicating to and who also understands the best communication vehicles for delivering information and for mobilizing and reinforcing behavior modifications;
- subject matter experts to deliver the necessary change outcomes to achieve the change goals;
- a learning and development specialist to design and deliver any necessary training to facilitate and reinforce the behavior modifications necessary to achieve the change goals;
- a change manager who works with all of these individuals to maintain alignment and clarity on the change goals, tracks the performance of change metrics and the progress against the change plan, keeps change leadership and other stakeholders engaged, and maintains the appropriate pacing and forward momentum on the change initiative.

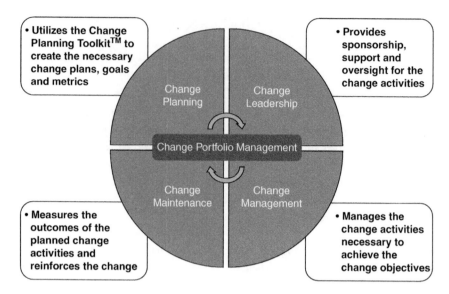

Figure 17.1 The Five Keys to Successful Change™

Change management is important to the success of your change effort, but as a reminder there are five keys to successful organizational change shown in figure 17.1:

1. change planning
2. change leadership
3. change management
4. change maintenance
5. change portfolio management

In a well-designed business, a project manager should operate under the direction of a change manager, who works with a distributed change leadership team to execute a plan built by the change planning team in collaboration with the portfolio management, business architecture, strategy, and innovation teams.

Most Organizations Suck at Change

One of the reasons many organizations are so bad at change is that they are not structured for change. While most people would agree that change is a constant, it is however not a constant focus for most businesses. Instead most organizations focus on the day-to-day business, and they focus on executing a portfolio of projects, ideally on time and on budget. In some cases, projects may incorporate some elements of change management (usually too late in the process) and ignore change planning, change leadership, change maintenance, and change portfolio management. Most companies focus on delivering a set of new systems, products, and services, and the ROI they may return instead of consciously architecting the organization for change (starting with changing customer behaviors, including wants/needs).

As a result, most organizations suck at change. And ultimately, most organizations suck at innovation because they suck at change.

Changes in customer behaviors and the marketplace (including regulation and competition) should inform the changes in employee, supplier, and partner behaviors, changes that are needed to keep a company's product and service offerings aligned with customers' evolving wants and needs. Innovation and continuous improvement efforts are crucial to maintaining this alignment.

As you see in figure 17.2, companies architected for change are constantly adjusting their strategy based on changes in the marketplace and changes in customer behavior. This then drives the identification of changes in the business architecture necessary to support any changes in strategy to maintain the optimum levels of competitiveness and customer connection. Any necessary changes in the architecture of the business (new or updated capabilities or competencies) then will lead to modifications of the portfolio of change initiatives and projects (and remember that every project is a change effort). These projects will consist of innovation initiatives and efforts to create positive changes in the operations of the business. The change planning discipline and the use of the Change Planning Toolkit™ will allow the business to collaboratively and visually plan each change effort and prepare the plans for the change management and change leadership teams to execute with help from the project planning, project management, and change maintenance professionals in the organization.

Figure 17.2 Architecting the Organization for Change

Capital C Change versus Lowercase C Change

As we look at managing change there is no doubt that change efforts fall rather messily into either into the capital C change bucket (programs focused on innovation, merger integration, restructuring, business transformation, or major system implementations) or the lowercase C change bucket (projects focused primarily on delivering process or system improvements). Capital C changes, as you can see, are typically programs (a collection of projects), and lowercase C changes usually are discrete projects with shorter timelines.

This difference in size is usually accompanied by a difference in scope and duration, and this influences the necessary investments in change planning, change leadership, change management, change maintenance, and change portfolio management activities. Because lowercase C change is typically smaller, organizations usually do not invest in anything more than basic project management, and this means that change management activities crucial to successful adoption are either addressed only marginally or ignored completely. In some organizations, surprisingly, this happens even with some capital C change efforts. This underinvestment in proactive change planning, cross-functional change leadership, change planning, change maintenance, and change portfolio management ultimately is what leads to the high failure rates associated with project and change program execution. For example, a 2007 email survey by *Dr. Dobbs Journal* had 586 respondents and "70 percent of respondents had been involved in a project they knew would fail right from the start."–[1] Effective change planning using the Change Planning Toolkit™, along with the active use of change leadership, change management, change maintenance, and change portfolio management is intended to help drive this number as close to zero as possible.

More on Project Management versus Change Management

Some people have described change management as the people side of change and project management as the technical side, and while this is partly true, it is only because the change management function oversees both the people side *and* the technical side. That is, while project planning/management focuses on achieving the technical outcomes of the change effort, change management also directs the behavior planning/management and communications planning/management necessary to create a successful change effort (with input and involvement/support from the change leadership team). You may notice in figure 17.2 that we've broken out communications planning/management out away from project planning/management. The reason for this is that in a change effort (which every project actually is), communications require extra care and different skills than those most project managers possess (i.e., segmentation, targeting, selection of medium and channel, etc.).

Summary

In this chapter we saw that in my model of successful organizational change and effective architecture for change, there are five components of successful organizational change:

1. change planning
2. change leadership
3. change management
4. change maintenance
5. change portfolio management

These five components are necessary whether you are working on a capital C change effort (a larger program with multiple projects) or a lowercase C change effort (a discrete project with a shorter timeline). When all these components are taken care of, your chances of failure should decline considerably.

We also examined the relationship between organizational change and project management in detail and saw that project management is a component of change management, not the other way around.

Finally, it is important to highlight that project planning/management is but one component of change planning/management along with behavior planning/management and communications planning/management.

Guest Expert

Dion Hinchcliffe (@dhinchcliffe)

Dion Hinchcliffe is chief strategy officer at Adjuvi. He is a well-known business strategist, enterprise architect, book author, frequent keynote speaker, analyst, and transformation consultant.

www.adjuvi.com

How Companies Are Discovering New Pathways for Digital Transformation

During the past 20 years, with the advent of the Internet, leaders of organizations have been seeking to develop meaningful business initiatives in the emerging digital channels. The desire has been to combine technology, online networks, and people with organizations' products and services. In the early days these efforts consisted primarily of moves into e-commerce and online advertising.

The goal for moving into digital was clear. Businesses could access vital new markets, and the technology would spur innovation and growth, all by mapping the old industrial world onto the new digitally connected one. In the early days, as organizations and the Internet matured and ideas became better adapted to the corporate world, discussions moved to fundamentally reimagining organizations to become digitally native *at their core*. This meant rethinking everything, even which business models to employ and why. This profound conversation created the digital transformation movement, which is perhaps today's most significant and fastest growing trend in business and technology.

Digital transformation is about holistic and meaningful adaptation of organizations to modern technologies and operating environments. Pervasive digitization of every part of our organizations' products and services is the new normal, including transformations in employee, partner, and customer engagement and the application of innovative business models and potent new ways of managing and working. These days, the very nature of business is being examined in digital terms, including the purpose and core mission of our organizations.

For those on the frontlines of the change, the past few years have been a rather thrilling time to be in business. There's still time for this transformation to be guided and shaped in many organizations. It's no longer an exaggeration to say there is more potential and opportunity for an organization right now than there

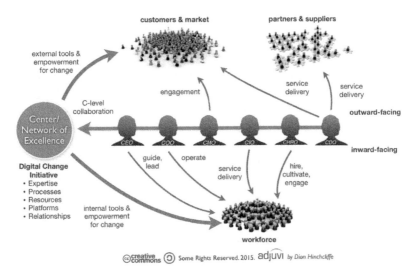

Figure 17.1.1   Collaborative C-Level Leadership Key to Digital Transformation

has been any time in corporate history. But too many organization leadship teams are struggling with how to best adopt today's disruptive advances and fundamentally alter the way they do business to match today's digital operating environment (see figure 17.1.1).

In this view, we are not alone. The *Harvard Business Review* recently noted[1] that typical large-scale transformation success rates still hover at only around 30 percent. That's grim news for those yet to build the digital bridge from their fading operating models to the new models required to succeed in today's world.

The Key: Collaboration Between the C-Suite and Networks of Change Agents

For years, it was difficult to discern why organizations were having so much trouble taking new paths to the future. Aging corporate structures are among the primary reasons. However, it's very hard to change fundamentals skills and the overall culture in large organizations. The rapid a rate of external digital change is forcing organizations to design for constant change. Current bureaucracies and hierarchies are too inflexible, and corporations must augment or even replace them with self-organizing networks. One example is the infamous "holacracy" experiment underway at online retailer Zappos.

However, none of the above represents the largest obstacle to digital transformation in most organizations. Instead, the root of the problem is actually the way organizations structure themselves to apportion responsibilities and wield leadership for digital change; in most cases they *mistakenly choose to divide it up.*

In recent years, as the digital transformation imperative became obvious even to the casual observer, the ownership for change has landed squarely in the lap of C-suite leaders as a core existential issue. Previously, most digital change has resulted from the efforts of change agents in the business units of organizations. These forward-thinking individuals, typically struggling to drive change lower down in the organization, have long been jousting with entrenched powers invested in the traditional business of the organization. These change agents have been pushing back steadily against the naysayers, the perennial skeptics, those beholden to the status quo, and those affected negatively by the major changes that now must take place in most organizations.

Digital Transformation Efforts Remain Fragmented

So what's the real obstacle to change today? As digital/social transformation has arrived at the C-suite and the board level, the issue of how to change and who is responsible for change has remained fragmented at the highest levels of organizational leadership. The chief information officer (CIO), chief digital officer (CDO), and chief marketing officer (CMO) typically all have partial ownership over large elements of digital transformation, and the chief human resources officer (CHRO) often owns the human transformation that goes with it. Other C-suite members usually have overlapping responsibilities with this group as well, which means that transformation efforts get fragmented and filtered through different priorities and worldviews with no central unifying force.

Thus, the core problem plaguing digital change is the artificial fragmentation created in many organizations, ultimately leaving nobody in charge. This issue goes well beyond the tug-of-war between CIOs and CMOs that is so hotly debated these days:

- Today's CIOs are in charge of developing the connected infrastructure for social business, digital workplace, digital business, etc., but not of the human component.
- CMOs are in charge of connecting with customers via all available channels, but through a vast digital infrastructure they largely do not create or own.
- CHROs are in charge of employee engagement as well as of approaches for recruiting, hiring, and performance management, but not of the technology involved or of those who are not employees.
- And chief operating officers (COO) are in charge of getting results (efficiency, performance) from employees for the business.

Such a strict domain focus in today's interconnected world is making it very difficult for organizations to create consistent, integrated, and well-managed digital transitions. So, if no single leader has responsibility for the whole process of digital transformation, including the technologies and connected participants (customers, workers, partners, and the marketplace), how can we best determine who should be responsible?

There is evidence from early efforts we can draw on. Thus far, the world has largely witnessed disjointed digital change in organizations. Existing parochial changes are primarily inward-only (CIO, COO, and CHRO), outward-only (CMO), employee-only (CHRO), tech-only (CIO), or business-only (lines of business, chief financial officer [CFO]). This federated approach, as we've now seen for the past few years, does not produce real transformation. Instead, we must remember that social has always been possible without digital, and so digital and social business are very much part of a single holistic continuum and must be addressed that way by organizations.

Examples of the fragmented, inefficient, and ineffective approach to change are everywhere. One can examine almost any large organization today and find the following:

- two separate social media initiatives (one facing inward and one outward);
- human resources (HR) working on employee engagement in isolation from the technology even though it's generally known they're deeply intertwined;

So, what is the solution?

There is one model clearly emerging and outperforming other new approaches, such as famous model of bimodal IT that is advocated by the top IT analyst firm, Gartner. At the root of many major digital success stories today seems to be effective collaboration among all those in the C-suite, driving coordinated change in combination with a program that enlists as many participants as possible from throughout an organization to drive the change in day-to-day activities.

Of course, rates of change across an organization for any large initiative will always vary based on the necessity to manage dependencies, risks, and resource availability. Paradoxically, holistic change does not occur in a single burst organization-wide. Instead, it is adaptive, more in the manner of new organizational practices, such as agile methods or dynamic "pods" of teams, with people coming together for the purpose of change and applying iterative approaches in parallel with active feedback loops at scale across an organization.

The Network of Excellence: A New Model for Successful Digital Change

So far, the latest case studies and success stories emerging from organizations such as the Federal Communications Commission, Houghton-Mifflin-Harcourt, and IBM bear out the perspective that digital change is a process that succeeds most effectively when those in the C-suite:

- work together closely,
- pool resources,

- mutually reinforce each other,
- empowers change agents wherever in the organization they may be,
- drives change consistently through a well-defined (but agile) process that—and this is the key—drives widespread empowerment across the organization.

There is evidence that all of this is a natural evolution from earlier forms of more targeted, high-speed technology change. Recent years have seen the maturation of the increasingly popular center of excellence (CoE) model, which originally evolved in response to a desire for faster technology change. But CoEs tended to mimic the IT departments and other business units they served by quickly exhausting centrally allocated resources for change. The model is still a good one, but it tends to put experts, staff, and knowledge into an overly central whole, instead of involving as many in the organization as are willing to change.

The new model doesn't have a widely accepted name yet, but for convenience let's call it a network of excellence (NoE) that is more empowered and made up of distributed change agents who are supported by centralized change and digital transformation experts/leadership. These networks are pooling expertise and resources to be applied quickly when a change agent is ready to move forward. It's a model that can enlist more of an organization's resources and make it possible to do more in parallel.

As new models emerge for digital transformation, such as the NoE, we must also remind ourselves why this happens. The hard data from the *MIT Technology Review*[2] and elsewhere says that technology change is now relentless and destroying companies that fail to adapt to their new digital operating environments. At the same time, organizations can be heartened by the fact that they are at long last able to adjust their digital priorities this year to deal with these critical obstacles.

While there will likely be more new models for effective transformation emerging naturally from the pressures organizations are dealing with today, the main problem is that old models for change have resulted in low success rates. The network of excellence model is the only model consistently emerging across industries, geographies, and organizations of widely varying cultures that can engage enough of the organization, help it learn faster, and can support a fast enough rate of change. The NoE model applies the same ideas that make our new digital operating models so compelling and powerful, namely, networks of people sharing interests (such as a desire for change). It should be underscored again how suitable and well-aligned this apparently new model is with the digital future that is already here.

CHAPTER 18

The Future of Change

Gabriella
(Age 10)

"The art of prophecy is difficult, especially with respect to the future."—Mark Twain

T he future requires change. This self-evident truth has led to efforts inside organizations to increase financial agility and organizational agility in a quest to not only decrease time to market, but time to transform as well. The organizations that succeed and thrive in the future will not be those that are built to last, but those that are built to change. This means enabling organizations to quickly react and adapt to changing market conditions. This change requires continuous restructuring the business and realigning the entire organization so as to always optimally serve customers' wants and needs *better* than the competition, even as those customer wants and needs continue to change.

Eight Principles of Continued Change Success

As the pace of change accelerates and the nature of change continues to evolve, the most forward-thinking, adaptable, and successful organizations will be the ones taking a slightly different approach to change than their struggling competitors. Companies able to cope with the pace and magnitude of future changes will approach change using the following Eight Principles of Continued Change Success (see figure 18.1).

1. Expected

Let's face it, the idea of "built to last" has become "built to fail." Data helps create information that becomes knowledge, which in turn helps uncover insights that

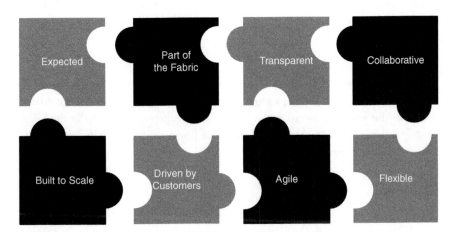

Figure 18.1   Eight Principles of Continued Change Success

are turned into innovations that disrupt ecosystems and create change. With the resources now available people are combining idea fragments into inventions, prototypes, market tests, and global launches faster than ever before. Change has gone from being surprising to expected, and organizations that expect continued success, will expect change.

2. Part of the Fabric

One reason many organizations struggle to achieve success with their change efforts is that they don't view change as expected have not rebuilt their organization to provide the resources, education, and infrastructure successful change efforts require. Successful organizations expect change and commit resources to effectively planning, leading, managing, and maintaining their desired change outcomes. This includes building and maintaining a business architecture so leaders know what the fabric of their organization looks like now and in the future. To make successful change a part of your company's culture requires the use of heat maps as part of your change portfolio; these maps identify the parts of your organizational fabric that are overheating with too much change and too few resources (also known as change saturation).

3. Transparent

As the pace and impact of change increase, the need for transparency will grow. Less transparency leads to diminished trust, lower engagement, decreased productivity, and less innovation. Increasing visibility and communications around potential changes in the needs and wants of the customer, shifts in the business architecture, etc. can actually lead to higher employee engagement, greater accountability, and more input from employees into the change planning process; this will lead to greater success in achieving desired change outcomes. Application of Agile Kanban methods to your change efforts can help with transparency. My Change Planning Toolkit™ includes an Agile Change Management Kanban template you can use.

4. Collaborative

Making the process of change more transparent will naturally lead to increased collaboration, but by introducing a more visual and more collaborative change process broadly—for example, by using the tools in the toolkit—you can make the initiation of a change effort feel more natural, more human. This will help get everyone all on the same page for change.

5. Flexible

Flexibility and agility are both on the list and in figure 18.1, but they are different. Flexibility refers to the ability to stretch resources and the organization to do different things; agility designates the ability to change direction quickly. For example, in automobile manufacturing the move away from assembly line workers who only knew how to do one task toward work teams with rotating responsibilities was a way of introducing more flexibility. This move also led to more employee engagement in the work process and to increased quality and production. Many organizations have gone too far in their push to maximize the potential output from each employee. Optimizing for maximum output often leads to rigidity, which is the enemy of change, and the antithesis of flexibility. To make the organization more flexible, leaders must restructure the organization to allow for more resource mobility and slack time. For example, Blockbuster got really good at running video stores, and Borders was really good at running book stores, but both companies are out of business in part because they lacked the flexibility to adapt to the changing wants and needs of customers.

6. Agile

In the previous section we defined agility as the ability to change direction quickly. One of the keys to success in building organizational agility is developing the ability to test and learn and kill. The last one is the hardest for most people and is the enemy of both innovation and change. To be an agile organization, your company must be able to identify and kill those efforts that are not delivering the desired outcomes and only retain those that are producing the progress or results required. Resources are not unlimited, and resources given to zombie projects deprive projects that could transform the organization. The other key to creating agility in the organization comes from breaking down project-based work into smaller, but still complete, value added work packages with more frequent decision points. Lean startup methods, such as minimum viable product (MVP) and pivot, support this approach, as does the Business Model Canvas. As the pace of change accelerates, agility becomes important because you are more likely to have to change your change so you don't end up solving a problem that was relevant and important at the beginning of the effort, but now no longer is either.

Increased agility is achieved by establishing the right balance between flexibility and fixedness, and is highlighted in the Organizational Agility Framework in figure 18.2. Too much flexibility and it will take too long to make decisions and changes. Too much fixedness and you will suffer from organizational rigidity.

7. Driven by Customers

Companies increasingly talk about being customer-focused, customer-centric, or customer-driven. Usually when companies start throwing this terminology around, they are trying to show that they are focused on providing a superior level of customer service, but the pivot companies built for continued change success will want to make is the pivot from customer service to serving customers. This may seem like a subtle distinction, but it is actually quite large, because companies that are truly serving

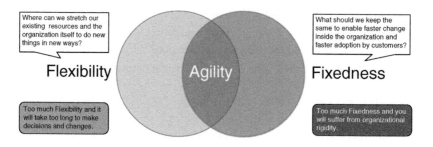

Increased **Organizational Agility** is achieved by establishing the right balance between **Flexibility** and **Fixedness.**

Figure 18.2   Organizational Agility Framework

customers realize that customers give them permission to exist. And it is by focusing relentlessly on understanding and executing upon what their customers give them permission to do that companies can ensure their continued existence and maximize their revenues. Because adoption is key, companies driven by customers realize that customer permissions communicate what the latter will adopt from a company— that is, what they trust a company to sell to them and also what they want a company to sell to them. For example, do you want Honda to sell you perfume? What about a lawn mower? What about a blender? Too often we focus on what we want to sell to customers instead of what they want to buy from us. Making that switch in the mind-set of the organization can make it more capable of change.

8. Built to Scale

The brain has two hemispheres. The left brain is known for logical reasoning, the right is best known for creativity and experimentation. People achieve their greatest success by bringing the strengths of both together. Organizations are no different. The key is to maintain areas of the organization that are good at creativity and experimentation and other areas that are good at organizing and scaling complexity and then maintain a strong bridge between the two. This is not easy, but to survive your organization must create space for increased experimentation and get better at scaling the successful experiments in order to better satisfy the ever-changing wants and needs of their customers.

The Learning Organization

For an organization to accelerate its organizational agility in response to the increasing pace of change, the organization must openly embrace and communicate a desire to continuously learn. This includes building "test and learn" into the culture of the organization while focusing on learning from both failures and successes. One of the most common questions in a learning organization will always be: What did we learn?

Organizational learning is an investment that always generates a return. In some ways learning is like interest, it compounds over time. There are many ways for organizations to reinforce a learning culture. These include the obvious initiatives driven by the human resources (HR) department:

- learning portal
- leadership programs
- classroom training
- educational reimbursement
- budget for employees to attend relevant conferences and seminars

Supporting individual learning can help increase the knowledge capital of the organization, and in this context the faster individuals can learn, the more open and capable of change their organization becomes.

But an organization can play the role of accelerator by helping to speed up the learning of individuals by helping to create connections and sharing, for example through:

- internal internship programs like Cisco's
- lunch 'n' learns (come learn about what a particular job or department does)
- town hall Q&A luncheons with executives
- speaker series
- book clubs
- guilds (enabling people with the same job to connect and share ideas and best practices and learnings)
- communities of interest (enabling people with a shared interest in a particular capability to connect and share)
- cross-Functional bottom-up innovation communities, such as Qualcomm's Flux
- A digital portal to give employees a place to share improvement or change idea fragments that can be shaped collaboratively into more complete ideas the organization can consider adopting;
- hack days focused on a particular challenge the organization is facing or a new customer want or need
- more widely shared voice of the customer information so people can learn more about the customers
- groups of employees enabled to take approved time off together to focus on advancing an idea that bubbled up from a bottom-up innovation community, an idea submission site, or a hack day via an "innovation vacation" that can be scheduled with the assistance of HR and affected managers;
- Face-to-face meetups of virtual teams funded at least once a year, an approach utilized by Automattic, the creators of Wordpress.

Companies seeking to accelerate their pace of change should identify and hire people who are passionate about lifelong learning, because those individuals will be more likely to embrace and create continuous change. After all, the faster your employees are learning and growing, the faster your organization can grow and learn. This is especially true if your organization is functioning as an accelerator using some of the methods described here, instead of acting as a brake.

Through the support of individual learning, the acceleration of learning through organization-sponsored connection and sharing, and the creation of a test and learn mentality through visible support for more prototyping and experimentation in the organization, you will start see that you are not only creating more of a learning organization but also an increase in organizational agility and flexibility.

Summary

In this chapter we looked at the power of the learning organization and how the Eight Principles of Continued Change Success give organizations a manageable number of principles to focus on in coping with the accelerating pace of change.

As a reminder, the Eight Principles of Continued Change Success are:

1. expected
2. part of the fabric
3. transparent
4. collaborative
5. flexible
6. agile
7. driven by customers
8. built to scale

Build a learning organization based on the Eight Principles of Continued Change Success, and you will be able to succeed in an environment dominated by accelerating, unrelenting change. Choose not to, and eventually your competitor(s) or new market entrants who do this will happily take your market share.

Change is all around us, and every day we change the world, whether we realize it or not. The only question is: Will you change your world for better or for worse today? Embrace the change!

Note: To access the Change Planning Canvas™ and selected tools from the Change Planning Toolkit™ and other resources, please visit www.charting-change.com.

Guest Expert

Rohit Talwar (@fastfuture)

Rohit Talwar is a global futurist and CEO of Fast Future Research and Fast Future Publishing. He is the editor of *The Future of Business,* published in June 2015.

www.FastFuture.com and **www.FastFuturePublishing .com**

Dancing with Disruption: Forces Shaping the Future of Business

Venturing into Uncertainty

Our world is being transformed by rapid advances in science and technology that are touching every aspect of our lives. We only have to look around us to see just how much can change in a relatively short time. So what changes could these developments bring about for life as we know it in the next ten years? What are the questions that these developments raise for businesses as they try to plan their strategies for navigating an uncertain and rapidly evolving future?

Below I take a brief look at ten scenarios exploring how some of these developments could come together and impact different aspects of our world. I also highlight brands and individuals that could play a significant role in shaping the future. I close with a discussion of ten questions that organizations are increasingly being forced to address as they try to prepare for the future of business.

Transformational Developments on the Horizon

Our lives have been shaped by developments most of us couldn't have imagined a decade ago. For example, handheld devices, such as smartphones and tablets, now allow us to have live video conversations with our friends, translate instantaneously between multiple languages, watch full-length videos, and monitor various aspects of our health, from blood pressure to oxygen flow and stress levels. Moreover, 3D printing is now available in nearly every home and is being used to create everything from blood cells to entire houses, and new aircraft such as the A380 can carry over 800 passengers on a single flight.

As we look ahead, the decade could be shaped by advances in nanotechnology, information technology, vertical farming, artificial intelligence, robotics, 4D printing, supersmart materials, neuroscience, and the biological sciences including genetics. Here are ten scenarios that we can see arising out of these developments:

1. Human 2.0

Human augmentation will accelerate in the next decade. By 2025 we will be witnessing a new breed of human 2.0 and 3.0 who have "hacked" their own bodies. Mind-enhancing drugs are already a reality, and we can now have supersmart prosthetic limb replacements that have greater functionality than the limbs we were born with. Both fields will continue to progress, and we will see genetic treatments to eliminate conditions such as extreme rage and obesity.

All of these enhancements will be monitored and managed 24/7 by a variety of wearable technologies and devices implanted into our bodies. These will help us track every vital sign and link directly to both our own handheld devices and to monitoring services provided by our health care providers. Indeed, 3D printing already allows us to create replacement body parts. The evolution to 4D printing will enable the manufacture of body parts that can self-assemble and adapt their shape and properties over time—giving us limbs that could reinforce themselves as we age.

2. National Sovereignty

The map of the globe will change as a result of economic forces. Many smaller and poorer countries may find it impossible to cope on their own with the accelerating pace of change and the cost of keeping up with a globally connected planet. By 2025, we could see 20–25 country mergers as "at risk" nations seek to come together to create the critical economic strength and attract the investment required to serve their populations and compete in the hyperconnected era.

3. Corporate Giants

As many as 50 percent of the Fortune 500 index of the largest publicly listed companies in 2025 will come from firms that did not even exist in 2015. We will see an ever-increasing number of so-called exponential companies that achieve rapid rates of growth by using science and technology to disrupt old industries and create new ones. For example, the taxi app Uber didn't even exist in 2008. and in 2015 was valued at over $40 billion; a number of new technology-based businesses, such as AirBnB and Snapchat, achieved valuations of over $10 billion in 2015.

Many more megagrowth players will emerge in sectors, such as driverless cars, 3D and 4D printing, genetics, and web-based applications and services that we can't even imagine today. Some argue that the notion of public stock markets will have been transformed by more efficient online crowdfunding platforms and the widespread use of digital currencies that effectively create a single global monetary system.

4. Financial Services

By 2025, the financial services landscape will have been transformed by digital currencies like bitcoin, blockchain technology, open markets, and a wave of new providers offering crowd-based solutions for everything from insurance to equity investment and commercial financing. These community platforms will let us lend to and invest in each other—bypassing the existing providers of saving, business investment, loans, and personal insurance.

5. Brain Uploading

By 2025 we will have mapped how the human brain works, and technology companies will be competing to host the "backup" of our brains online. Three major projects in Europe, the United States, and China are currently involved in major research activities to understand how the brain stores information and memories. This will ultimately allow us to create memory backups with the information stored remotely via an online service provider in exactly the same way many of us already store the data on our computers and mobile devices.

6. Immersivity

By 2025 technology advances will give rise to new immersive live and virtual leisure experiences. For example, we will be able to become participants in live action adventure games from Roman battles to rerunning the Olympic 100 meters final with robots performing the roles of the other contestants.

7. Mixed Reality Living

The boundaries between virtual and physical worlds will have disappeared by 2025 as we place multiple layers of digital sensory augmentation over our physical environment. Augmented and virtual reality will have advanced to the point where we can stimulate all our senses over the Internet and via our handheld devices. For example, when booking a hotel, these developments would enable us to feel the bed linens, taste the food in the restaurant, and smell the bath products—all from a device in the palm of our hands.

8. Robotics

The replacement of humans by robots in manufacturing has been taking place for two decades, and it is now spreading to a wide range of other sectors such as elder care, crop spraying, and warehouse management. By 2025 robots will have entered every aspect of human life and will be commonplace and perform functions as diverse as nursing, complex surgery, policing, and security; they will work in construction, retail, and hotels in service roles. All of the major vehicle manufacturers are working on autonomous or driverless cars, which is a form of robot we will see coming to market in the next few years.

9. Artificial Intelligence

Breakthroughs in Artificial Intelligence (AI) are accelerating with the development of computer software that has the capacity to mimic humans' ability to learn and adapt over time to changing circumstances. AI is already in widespread use in applications, such as sat nav systems, airplane autopilots, assessing credit and loan applications in financial services, automated call centers, and health care diagnoses. Advances in AI will gather momentum in the next decade. For example, by 2025 the interfaces of all our devices from phones to computers, cars, and home appliances will be highly intelligent and adaptive; they will learn from our behaviors and choices and be able to anticipate our needs.

10. Internet of Life

In the next decade more than 100 billion objects from smartphones to street lamps and cars will be connected together via a vast Internet of everything (IoE). This will impact every aspect of our lives—for example, this development could transform the criminal justice system. By 2025, evidence in a court case will include data taken from body cameras and microphones and sensors in everyday objects, such as clothing, furniture, and even our coffee cups; these objects will prove exactly what happened and who was present at the scene of a crime.

Who Are the Future Makers?

The last twenty years have seen the emergence of "born digital" innovators and entrepreneurs who see every problem and opportunity as something that can be addressed by capturing the data and applying the right software algorithms. Hence, established players, such as Google, see no bounds to their ambitions, whether in artificial intelligence, driverless cars, or extending human life expectancy. They are investing heavily in these and many other areas. These new digital masters of the universe believe no problem is beyond them; for example, Facebook believes it could transform health care and banking while Apple wants to provide the interface and ecosystem through which we manage our lives.

Pioneers are emerging in sectors as diverse as food, housing, and health care who believe they can deliver breakthroughs that will tackle fundamental human needs and challenges. For example, Elon Musk and others like him are stretching our imagination with ventures in areas such as colonizing space and driverless green vehicles. In politics, Syriza in Greece and the Pirate Party in Iceland are pursuing fresh new ideas on how future economic systems might operate.

Critical Questions for Business

In the face of these developments, we see businesses increasingly wrestling with some fundamental questions that could shape medium-term and long-term strategies:

1. Automation and Commoditization

How do we compete and make a profit in a world where automation and digitization are shortening business cycles, accelerating change, and driving the commoditization of many goods and services?

2. Rising Life Expectancy

How do we manage and motivate a workforce that could range in age from 16 to 90 years as people's life expectancy rises, and they are forced to keep working to survive?

3. Human Augmentation

What's the impact on our business and the commercial opportunity arising from people using scientific advances to enhance the performance of their brains and bodies?

4. Resource Management

How will we produce our products when scarce natural resources run out or are rationed?

5. Exponential Thinking

Can we transfer exponential thinking from the technology world to other domains to address the problems of scarcity in essentials from food and water to rare earth metals?

6. Smart Machines

How close is the day when smart technologies such as artificial intelligence (AI) could replace almost our entire workforce?

7. The Automated Enterprise

What could the fully automated company of tomorrow look like and who will buy our goods and services if technology is eliminating jobs at every level of the workforce?

8. Tomorrow's Customer

If technology replaces humans in the workplace in ever-increasing numbers, how will they feed themselves and purchase goods and services? Will we need a universal basic income and how will it be funded?

9. Rethinking the Financial System

How might the nature of money and financial systems evolve, and what impact could possible transformations have on our business?

10. The Future of Business

What would be the driving purpose and societal role of business in a world being transformed by all these forces of change?

None of these questions have simple or straightforward answers. The decisions we make will have diverse influences depending on our outlook on money, technology, humanity, and the role of business in society in the decade to come. This promises to be a challenging, exciting, developmental, and experimental decade as we learn and feel our way through to the strategies and models of the future.

For more on these topics, be sure and check out *The Future of Business*[1] (www.fastfuturepublishing.com), published in June 2015. This fast-track publishing project was completed in just 19 weeks. The book's 60 chapters draw on the views of 62 future thinkers from 21 countries to explore the drivers of change and how business could evolve in response over the next two decades.

Guest Expert

Ayelet Baron (@ayeletb)

Ayelet Baron is a futurist helping to build thriving twenty-first-century organizations with leaders consciously driving a shared purpose. Ayelet is a keynote speaker and author whose purpose is to open people's minds and hearts about what's possible when we perform our lifework in abundance.

www.AyeletBaron.com

Change Is Abundant in the Twenty-First Century

Change is constant and a reality of today's world. We live in a time when entire economies, industries, and organizations are reshaping. And yet, many people in organizations are under the illusion that change is a program that can neatly be tied with a bow. In reality, change is not only part of the twenty-first century but also a way of life for most organizations that want to remain relevant.

What Is Change?

The simple definition of change is any time a person's expectations are disrupted. Consider the case of an organization based in San Diego that decides to introduce a collaborative Enterprise 2.0 platform and shift people to working online. For Karuna, who lives in Hong Kong, this is a welcome change, as she believes she can now be more connected to her colleagues and will have more information about what's going on in the organization. She is also excited that this may help bring the team closer together despite the cultural and time zone challenges they face.

However, for Peter, who works in headquarters, this is yet another "flavor of the month" initiative that will waste his time and force him to use one more online tool. Peter wonders how this will be different from last year's initiative, while Karuna is hopeful that the new tool will help reduce the time zone challenges and will help the team solve problems and have transparency regarding key decisions.

Why Change?

And we can all see how this story will end because of how it began. Our story began when the CEO of this global company asked the global head of operations, Bill, to look into this platform after attending a C-suite event where his biggest competitor presented that company's new platform. Bill begrudgingly looked into it and presented the business case for introducing this new collaborative online platform to improve internal communication.

A decision was made to pilot the platform and see how it goes. Bill's job was done at that point. IT was brought in and so was a consultant to drive the change management, and the internal communication function was asked to build a plan. The goal of the change was to successfully implement the new platform, which was the first mistake on the road to adoption. The change program became focused on the platform with no clear leadership or ownership as to why it is integral to the business. The communication was more about the platform than about how it will help drive results.

Who Is Accountable?

The challenge we have in many of today's organizations is that we are using antiquated management practices from an earlier century. In the twenty-first century, we need to lead with the business and shared purpose. People accept and internalize changes faster when there is alignment with the business. Leaders have become addicted to hiring change management experts (internally and externally) and believe these experts can come into an organization, wave their magic wand, and declare success of an initiative until the next program needs to be defined and executed. In essence, since executive sponsorship usually only lasts 24 hours (executives are constantly being asked to sponsor many changes without clear accountability to what that sponsorship means in terms of behavior), not enough focus and time is spent on making sure the leaders are using the platform, for example, and integrating it in their day-to-day work.

Lead with Business and Shared Purpose

In our story, while we asked the executives to sponsor the change, we failed to work with them to own and adopt it. The leaders in this organization were sabotaging the change they had initiated because they didn't believe in it and chose to delegate their responsibility to others. The world is not going to wait for an organization to get a program to change. In today's environment, leaders need to figure out what their key opportunities are and bring the right people together to make change happen with shared purpose.

Many organizations are increasingly introducing new technology for technology's sake. In the constant pursuit of keeping up and having the latest shiny objects, we have somehow lost touch with the business side of change.

There is huge resistance in the top layers of organizations that no one talks about or manages. We need to stop seeing the evolution of the business and every new program as a change initiative. People are resisting the constant introduction of more programs since they do not see the changes integrated into a clear shared purpose around the business outcome. They know that nine times out of ten, every new initiative will soon be forgotten. The bottom line: Many leaders find it painful to admit that the management model that predominates in most organizations is rooted in the nineteenth century. In twenty-first-century organizations, this old model simply no longer works; today, to remain relevant, organizations must be agile and flexible.

While change management was introduced in the twentieth century, those early programs were disconnected from the business, and they need to be put to rest. In a world of abundant opportunities to cocreate and collaborate, there is no room to have sponsors of initiatives. In the old world, a new initiative would pop up, and we would need to do some mapping and decide who the executive sponsor should be and then go "contract" with that person on his or her role as sponsor.

How do I know all of this? I was there when the change management movement started. Not only was I trained and certified in organizational change management, but I also went to work for one of the original change gurus in the late 1990s. And then, instead of remaining a change consultant, I joined a large high-tech company and integrated change in how we worked and drove business results globally. I became a business strategist and innovator who knew how to help organizations shift by helping leaders understand how to integrate the change into how we worked. There was no program required. When the CEO of Cisco Canada told me that he wanted to move Canada from the number six revenue-generating country for Cisco to number three, we built a business plan around that change and ended up taking the Canadian company to number two in revenue at $2 billion. When Cisco's CIO wanted to move IT from a vendor to a business partner, we integrated the goal into our work, and customer satisfaction jumped from 69 percent to 76 percent in two years. No sponsors, ambassador programs, or one-way communication programs were required.

Why People Resist Change

To deal with resistance and get people to accept change, we need to know what the top culprits are that get in the way. The first one is that people become comfortable in the way things are done today and don't want to risk the unknown. And often organizations reward people for doing what they are doing. They may promote innovation, but failure is usually not recognized as a positive, despite the claims of leaders. So why change? It's nice to hear messages about failure being useful, but if the leaders do not reinforce the message with positive activities, no one will want to be the first to fail. And change necessitates a leap of faith.

This brings us to the number one reason why people resist change. For those in organizations that are still stuck in the twentieth-century world of scarcity, fear is alive and well. And if a fear of failure is ingrained in the subconscious culture, people will be adverse to change, especially with so many possible negative outcomes. When we don't do a good job of integrating change into the business and telling a story about why it's critical to the business, there is no compelling reason for people to change how they get their work done. Let's take a look at how people think and act in twentieth century organizations versus twenty-first century organizations:

Twentieth-Century Organizations	Twenty-First – Century Organizations
Deficit mind-set: There is not enough	Abundance mind-set: We have enough
Competing	Collaborating
Sponsorship: ask leaders to sponsor the change	Conscious Leaders own and integrate the change into the business
Managed and delegated as a change program	Integrated into the business with strategic partners
One-way communication to audiences	Storytelling and conversations with communities
Resistance to change	Work and adapt to changing business needs
Measure activity	Measure impact

A New Mind-set to Help People Adopt Change

What is needed today is a new mind-set starting with leaders in organizations. Twenty-first-century leaders build community and bring people together around a shared purpose. They focus on what is possible and understand that change is constant and that they need to build organizations with two-way communication and conversations that engage people.

There are no standard best practices to follow when integrating change into the fabric of an organization. The process is about leaders consciously asking themselves some of the questions below and approach change with a mind-set of ownership instead of sponsorship and delegating it to someone else.

- *What is the business need to change?* If you have a clear answer to "why change" that is integrated into your business, people will be excited about being part of this new shift. They will not need to believe that the current way of doing things is the only way. They will not see the change as a fad or the flavor of the month.
- *Have you practiced empathy and truly listened?* If you understand and can empathize with what the people you are asking to change will need to do, you will build a targeted strategy. You will know what people fear, and you can have conversations (rather than one-way communication campaigns) to allay their concerns. People take steps toward the unknown when they believe that the risks of not changing are greater than those of moving in a new direction. Make sure that people are part of the change, as they need to know what's going on, especially if it impacts their work.

- *Do you have communities to tap into?* Instead of a traditional change strategy, you have an influencing strategy in place and know who the main people are that you need to have conversations with. Often you can create this influencing strategy by understanding your in-person and online community structure and tapping into the right conversations with the right people.

- *Are your leaders sharing stories?* Instead of creating traditional communication plans with audiences you need to communicate to, your leaders are openly sharing stories about the business change. Instead of talking about the need to innovate, the conversations are stories that exemplify innovating. The only time we have an audience is when we go to the theater to see a show or listen to a band. Successful organizations build communication plans that are two-way conversations.

- *What's the level of trust in your organization?* If people have a strong sense of trust, they will believe that they, or the organization, can competently transform. Trust comes only when it is safe for people to make changes. People want to share in the successes and/or failures of twenty-first-century leaders who are trusted for authenticity and agility. People feel safe in taking a leap of faith with such leaders.

- *Have you invested time in understanding the impact of the change on your people?* When we ask people to work in new ways, we need to provide them with a road map on what they can expect to change. It is hard for people who are used to a particular way of getting their work done to let go. They have been successful so far and have been rewarded for it. I recently did an empathy session with a leader who shared that he was trained never to go into a room if he doesn't have the answer. It was no surprise that he resisted collaborating openly in an online community where he would need to be vulnerable and not have all the answers. Most people love routine, and changing that is the definition of change. Every time we disrupt people's expectations—that is change.

- *Do people have the skills needed to change?* When we ask people to change, we need to make sure that we provide everyone with the opportunity to acquire any necessary new skills. People will not tell you that they don't have the skills needed, but if you listen with intent and empathy, you will clearly understand where you need to invest in building skills. And this investment is worth it now that change is built into your business model and will help your organization achieve its purpose. If the benefits and rewards for making the change are not worth the trouble, ask yourself why you are changing.

Change Is Abundant: It's Time to Navigate and Integrate

If you lead an twenty-first-century organization, you know that change is abundant. You don't feel scarcity and always look for opportunities and possibilities. Keep the view that "change is hard" and that you need a professional to drive it for you, and this view will definitely lead to failure. If you want to be a twenty-first century leader, you will instead have strategic partners who, like you, have skin in the game to achieve your shared purpose.

It's time to step off the command-and-control wheel and tap into people both inside and outside your organization. Connected networks and trusted communities become increasingly important in a world where more people are getting a voice and wanting to make a difference, in their work and in their life as a whole.

Notes

1 Changing Change

1. Richard Foster, "Creative Destruction Whips through Corporate America: An Innosight Executive Briefing on Corporate Strategy," Innosight.com, 2012, p. 2.
2. Manifesto for Agile Software Development, http://agilemanifesto.org.
3. Daryl Conner, The Four Kinds fo Burning Platforms, August 21, 2012, http://www.connerpartners.com/frameworks-and-processes/the-four-kinds-of-burning-platforms.
4. Eric Ries, *The Lean Startup*, Crown Business, 2011.

2 Planning Change

1. Queensland Government, https://www.business.qld.gov.au/business/employing/staff-development/managing-people-through-change/types-change.
2. David Straker, *Styles of Change*. 2006. Available from http://changingminds.org/disciplines/change_management/managing_change/style_change.htm (accessed July 18, 2015).
3. David Straker, *Change Strategy*. 2006. Available from http://changingminds.org/disciplines/change_management/planning_change/change_strategy.htm (accessed July 18, 2015).

BONUS FEATURE—NHS Case Study: Challenging Top-Down Change

1. The barriers to bottom-up change defined by the crowd (*Health Service Journal, Nursing Times,* NHS Improving Quality, "Change Challenge," March 2015).
2. The building blocks to bottom-up change (*Health Service Journal, Nursing Times,* NHS Improving Quality, "Change Challenge," March 2015).

4 Exploring Readiness for Change and Transitions

1. *The Enterprise of the Future.* IBM Global CEO Study. IBM, 2008.
2. Kurt Lewin. *Frontiers in Group Dynamics: Concept, Method and Reality in Social Science; Social Equilibria and Social Change.* Human Relations, June 1947.
3. William Bridges. *Managing Transitions.* Da Capo Lifelong Books, 1991.

4. Definition of "organization agility." BusinessDictionary.com.http://www.businessdictionary.com/definition/organizational-agility.html.

5   Envisioning the Desired State

1. Stuart Elliott, "THE MEDIA BUSINESS: Advertising; Microsoft Takes a User-Friendly Approach to Selling Its Image in a New Global Campaign," *New York Times*, November 11, 1994, http://www.nytimes.com/1994/11/11/business/media-business-advertising-microsoft-takes-user-friendly-approach-selling-its.html.

7   The Benefits of Change

1. Stephen Wagner and Lee Dittmar, "The Unexpected Benefits of Sarbanes-Oxley," *Harvard Business Review*, April 2006, https://hbr.org/2006/04/the-unexpected-benefits-of-sarbanes-oxley.

8   The People Side of Change

1. Geoffrey A Moore. *Crossing the Chasm*, HarperBusiness, 2006.
2. Roger Connors and Tom Smith. *Change the Culture, Change the Game*, Portfolio, 2012.
3. Ibid.

BONUS FEATURE—Matthew E. May (Guest Expert): Reverse Engineer Your Strategy by Asking "What Must Be True?"

1. Mike Berardino, "Mike Tyson Explains One of His Most Famous Quotes," *Sun Sentinel*, November 9, 2012, http://articles.sun-sentinel.com/2012-11-09/sports/sfl-mike-tyson-explains-one-of-his-most-famous-quotes-20121109_1_mike-tyson-undisputed-truth-famous-quotes.

11   Breaking It Down

1. John P Kotter. *Leading Change*. Harvard Business, 1996.

12   Now What (The Resource Challenge)

1. W. Chan Kim and Renee Mauborgne. *Blue Ocean Strategy: How to Create Uncontested Market Space and Make Competition Irrelevant*. Harvard Business Review Press, 2005.

BONUS FEATURE—Beth Montag-Schmaltz (Guest Expert): Bracing for the Next Wave of Change

1. "Capitalizing on Complexity. Insights from the 2010 IBM Global CEO Study." http://www-935.ibm.com/services/us/ceo/ceostudy2010/multimedia.html
2. *The High-Performance Workforce Study 2010.* http://www.bollettinoadapt.it/old/files/document/9906accenture_2010.PDF

3. Daniel Goleman, *Emotional Intelligence: Why It Can Matter More Than IQ*, Bantam Books, 1996.

4. *The 2011/2012 Talent Management and Rewards Study, North America*. Towers Watson, November 2011. https://www.towerswatson.com/Insights/IC-Types/Survey-Research-Results/2011/10/2011-Global-Talent-Management-and-Rewards-Study

5. John Medina, *Brain Rules: 12 Principles for Surviving and Thriving at Work, Home, and School*, Pear Press, 2009.

6. Ibid.

7. *Best Practices in Change Management*. Prosci, 2014. http://www.prosci.com/best-practices-in-change-management-2014-edition.html Prosci

8. Dennis McCafertty, "IT Management Slide Show: Why IT Projects Fail," *CIO Insight*, June 2010. http://www.cioinsight.com/c/a/IT-Management/Why-IT-Projects-Fail-762340

9. Cathy Farley and Walter Gossage, "The Agile Organization," Talent Management, July 2010. http://www.talentmgt.com/articles/the_agile_organization

13   Building the Case for Change

1. Roger Connors and Tom Smith, *Change the Culture, Change the Game*, Portfolio, 2012.

2. David Jacquemont, Dana Maor, and Angelika Reich, "How to Beat the Transformation Odds,"– http://mckinsey.com/insights/organization/how_to_beat_the_transformation_odds, April 2015.

3. Carl Binder. What's So New About the Six Boxes? White Paper, 2005. http://www.six-boxes.com/_customelements/uploadedResources/160039_SixBoxesWhatsSoNew.pdf

4. Joseph Grenny, Kerry Patterson, David Maxfield, Ron McMillan, and Al Switzler, *Influencer*, McGraw-Hill Education, 2013.

5. Roger Connors and Tom Smith, *Change the Culture, Change the Game*, Portfolio, 2012.

BONUS FEATURE—Brett Clay, PhD
(Guest Expert): Selling Change

1. John Kotter, *Our Iceberg Is Melting: Changing and Succeeding under Any Conditions*, St. Martins Press, 2006.

2. Self-Determination Theory. http://www.selfdeterminationtheory.org/theory/.

3. John Dudovskiy, "Lewin's Force-Field Theory of Change," Research Methodology, July 2, 2010, http://research-methodology.net/lewins-force-field-theory-of-change/.

4. Self-Determination Theory. http://www.selfdeterminationtheory.org/theory/.

5. Maslow's Hierarchy of Needs, Learning-Theories.com. http://www.learning-theories.com/maslows-hierarchy-of-needs.html.

6. Self-Determination Theory. http://www.selfdeterminationtheory.org/theory/.

BONUS FEATURE—Ty Montague and Rosemarie Ryan
(Guest Experts): StoryDoing® and
Organizational Change

1. Conrad Lisco, "The Key to Innovation: A Good Story," Innovation Insights, April 7, 2014, http://insights.wired.com/profiles/blogs/the-key-to-innovation-a-good-story#axzz3tDmL7Gql.

2. Gary Hamel, *The Future of Management*, Harvard Business Review Press, 2007.

15   Leading Change

1. John P. Kotter and Lorne A. Whitehead, *Buy-In: Save Your Idea from Getting Shot Down.* Harvard Business Review Press, 2010.

17   Project and Portfolio Management Are about Change

1. 2007 IT Project Success Rates Survey Results, Ambysoft, http://www.ambysoft.com/surveys/success2007.html.

BONUS FEATURE—Dion Hinchcliffe (Guest Expert): How Companies Are Discovering New Pathways for Digital Transformation

1. Ron Ashkenas, "We Still Don't Know the Difference Between Change and Transformation," *Harvard Business Review*, January 15, 2015.
2. David Rotman, "How Technology Is Destroying Jobs," *MIT Technology Review*, June 12, 2013.

BONUS FEATURE—Rohit Talwar (Guest Expert): Dancing with Disruption: Forces Shaping the Future of Business

1. Rohit Talwar, *The Future of Business: Critical Insights into a Rapidly Changing World from 60 Future Thinkers (FutureScapes) (Volume 1)*, Fast Future Publishing, 2015.

Bibliography

Balkin, Jack M. *The Laws of Change*. Schocken Books. 2002.

Bennis, Warren. *Organizing Genius*. Addison-Wesley. 1997.

Bennis, Warren G., Kenneth D. Benne, and Robert Chin. *The Planning of Change*. Holt, Rinehart and Winston. 1985.

Bodell, Lisa. *Kill the Company*. Bibliomotion. 2012.

Bridges, William, with Susan Bridges. *Managing Transitions*. Lifelong Books. 2009.

Brown, Tim. *Change by Design*. Harper Business. 2009.

Clay, Brett. *Selling Change*. Ariva Publishing. 2010.

Coerver, Harrison, and Mary Byers. *Race for Relevance*. ASAE. 2011.

Connors, Roger, and Tom Smith. *Change the Culture, Change the Game*. Portfolio, 2012.

Dobrowolski, Patti. *Drawing Solutions*. Creative Genius Press. 2014.

Gipple, Craig A., and Beth L. Evard. *Managing Business Change for Dummies*. Hungry Minds. 2001.

Green, Mike. *Change Management Masterclass*. Kogan Page. 2007.

Green, Mike, and Esther Cameron. *Making Sense of Change Management*. Kogan Page. 2009.

Grenny, Joseph, Kerry Patterson, David Maxfield, Ron McMillan, and Al Switzler. *Influencer*. McGraw-Hill Education, 2013.

Grenny, Joseph, Kerry Patterson, David Maxfield, Ron McMillan, and Al Switzler. *Change Anything: The New Science of Personal Success*. Business Plus. 2011.

Hammer, Michael, and Steven A. Stanton. *The Reengineering Revolution*. HarperBusiness. 1995.

Handy, Charles. *Gods of Management*. Oxford University Press. 1995.

Heath, Chip, and Dan Heath. *Switch*. Broadway Books. 2010.

Heath, Chip, and Dan Heath. *Made to Stick*. Random House. 2007.

Heffernan, Margaret. *Beyond Measure*. TED Books. 2015.

Heller, Robert. *Managing Change*. DK Publishing. 1998.

Holman, Peggy. *The Change Handbook: The Definitive Resource for Today's Best Methods for Engaging Whole Systems*. Berrett-Koehler Publishers. 2007.

Jacobs, Robert W. *Real Time Strategic Change*. Berret-Koehler Publishers. 1994.

Jarrett, Michael. *Changeability*. FT Prentice Hall. 2009.

Jennings, Jason. *The Reinventors: How Extraordinary Companies Pursue Radical Continuous Change*. Your Coach In A Box. 2012.

Jeston, John, and Johan Nelis. *Business Process Management*. Elsevier. 2008.

Kahan, Seth. *Getting Change Right*. Jossey-Bass, 2010.

Kanter, Rosabeth Moss. *Evolve!* HBR Press. 2001.

Kelley, Braden. *Stoking Your Innovation Bonfire*. Wiley & Sons. 2010.

Kleiner, Art. *The Age of Heretics*. Currency-Doubleday. 1996.

Kotter, John P. *The Heart of Change*. Harvard Business School Press. 2002.

Kotter, John P. *Leading Change*. Harvard Business School Press. 1996.

Kotter, John P. *Buy-In*. Harvard Business School Press. 2010.

Kriegel, Robert, and David Brandt. *Sacred Cows Make the Best Burgers*. Business Plus. 1996.

Mauborgne, Renee, and W. Chan Kim. *Blue Ocean Strategy*. Harvard Business Review Press, 2005.

Maurer, Rick. *Beyond the Wall of Resistance*. Bard Press. 2010.

Moore, Geoffrey. *Crossing the Chasm*. HarperBusiness, 2014.

Morrison, Ian. *The Second Curve*. Ballantine Books.1996.

Quinn, Robert E. *Deep Change*. Jossey-Bass. 1996.

Rath, Tom. *Eat Move Sleep: How Small Choices Lead to Big Changes*. Missionday. 2013.

Shenhar, Aaron J., and Dov Dvir. *Reinventing Project Management: The Diamond Approach to Successful Growth and Innovation*. Harvard Business School Press. 2007. Sibbet, David. *Visual Leaders*. Wiley. 2012.

Sibbet, David. *Visual Meetings: How Graphics, Sticky Notes, and Idea Mapping Can Transform Group Productivity*. Wiley. 2010.

Siebert, Al. *The Resiliency Advantage: Master Change, Thrive under Pressure, and Bounce Back from Setbacks*. Berrett-Koehler. 2005. Smith, Greg, and Ahmed Sidky. *Becoming Agile in an Imperfect World*. Manning. 2009.

Straker, David. *Styles of Change*. 2006. Available from http://changingminds.org/disciplines/change_management/managing_change/style_change.htm (accessed July 18, 2015).

Straker, David. *Change Strategy*. 2006. Available from http://changingminds.org/disciplines/change_management/planning_change/change_strategy.htm (accessed July 18, 2015).

Tushman, Michael L., and Charles A. O'Reilly III. *Winning Through Innovation*. Harvard Business School Press. 1997.

Ulrich, Dave. *Human Resource Champions*. Harvard Business School Press. 1997.

Watkins, Michael D. *The First 90 Days*. Harvard Business Review Press. 2013. (genesisadvisers.com)

Worley, Christopher G., Thomas Williams, and Edward E. Lawler III. *The Agility Factor*. Jossey-Bass. 2014.

About the Author

Braden Kelley, founder of Business Strategy Innovation, has been advising companies on how to increase their revenue and cut their costs since 1996. Braden is a thought leader on the topics of innovation and change and is working with clients to create innovative strategies, plan effective digital transformations, and build continuous innovation and change capabilities. He has maximized profits for companies while living and working in England, Germany, and the United States. Braden earned his MBA from top-rated London Business School.

But he hasn't always been an author and a business consultant. Braden served his country honorably in the United States Navy and traveled all around the Western Pacific. In his pre-MBA life he created Symantec's first web-based technical support and customer service as well as a digital tool for idea submissions to power 360-degree customer feedback. He then left to pursue a career as a knowledge management and collaboration consultant in Silicon Valley.

Braden is passionate about innovation and has written more than 500 articles for dozens of online publications (*Washington Post*, *Wired*, *The Atlantic*, LinkedIn, Texas Enterprise, and more), and many of his articles have been translated into Portuguese, Spanish, French, and Swedish. In addition, he has written white papers on several innovation topics for companies such as Innocentive, Planview, and Imaginatik.

Braden is the creator of the Change Planning Toolkit™, which contains dozens of powerful tools, including the Change Planning Canvas™.

In his spare time, Braden runs the world's most popular innovation community InnovationExcellence.com, which is home to more than 7,500 articles and video interviews with luminaries such as Dean Kamen, Kevin Roberts, John Hagel III, Seth Godin, Roger Martin, Dan Pink, and more. And last but not least, Braden is an innovation leader on Twitter (@innovate) and LinkedIn (http://linkedin.com/in/bradenkelley) with thousands of hard-earned followers.

Index